*Law*Basics

DELICT

AUSTRALIA
Law Book Co.
Sydney

CANADA and USA
Carswell
Toronto

HONG KONG
Sweet & Maxwell Asia

NEW ZEALAND
Brookers
Wellington

SINGAPORE and MALAYSIA
Sweet & Maxwell Asia
Singapore and Kuala Lumpur

*Law*Basics

DELICT

By

Gordon Cameron

Lecturer in Law at the University of Dundee

EDINBURGH
W. GREEN/Sweet & Maxwell
2002

Published in 2002 by

W. Green & Son Ltd
21 Alva Street
Edinburgh EH2 4PS

www.wgreen.co.uk

*Printed in Great Britain by Athenaeum Press,
Gateshead, Tyne & Wear*

No natural forests were destroyed to make this product;
Only farmed timber was used and replanted

A CIP catalogue record for this book is available from the British Library

ISBN 0414 012 33X

© W. Green & Son Ltd 2002

ACKNOWLEDGEMENTS

The author is grateful to those who have assisted in the preparation of this book. Particular thanks to Professor Niall Whitty of Edinburgh University and to Sue Moody, senior lecturer at Dundee, both of whom gave time to look at elements of the text which have benefited from their comments. Professor Colin Reid has been helpful as always and the text contains some of his suggestions as well as one or two useful insights from my colleague Robin White. Thanks also to Gillian Brand, honours student at Dundee, who gave up vacation time gratuitously to assist me in preparatory work. Thanks to staff at Green's and in particular to Neil McKinlay who demonstrated an exemplary level of understanding, patience and good humour waiting for each successive submission. Meanwhile I stole in piecemeal fashion the little time available to write this text from the persistent demands of teaching, admissions, original research, jumping through hoops and avoiding sticks while wondering what happened to all the carrots. I also acknowledge a general debt owed to Professor Joe Thomson of Glasgow University from whose writings I have derived much of my basic understanding of the subject. Finally, I am grateful to Dr Enid Marshall, retired from Stirling University, without whose "General Principles" I would never have passed my delict exam as a first year student in 1981.

CONTENTS

CONTENTS

TABLE OF CASES

1. INTRODUCTION

THE PLACE OF DELICT WITHIN THE LAW OF OBLIGATIONS

Delict is a branch of the law of obligations. The law of obligations is found within the wider sphere of private law, that is law that regulates relationships between private legal persons whether individual citizens or corporations. The law of obligations can be divided into three parts: the law of contract; the law of delict; and the law of unjust enrichment, also known as quasi-contract.

Parties take on contractual obligations by choice. Nobody can be forced into a valid contract against their will. Accordingly we say that contractual obligations arise *ex voluntate*, that is from the exercise of will. Delictual obligations, on the other hand, are imposed by law. We say that delictual obligations arise *ex lege*, that is by force of law. It is sometimes said that delictual obligations arise *ex culpa*, that is through fault. While this is true so far as common law obligations are concerned it may be noted that absolute or strict liability may be imposed by statute. In such cases *culpa* or fault on the part of the defender does not require to be established. Therefore delictual obligations under the common law arise *ex culpa*, but this is not true of all delictual obligations. Quasi-contractual obligations also arise *ex lege*. Where one party has been unjustly enriched at the expense of another, the law may impose an obligation to pay, or to return property in the absence of a contractual relationship between the parties.

A further category, quasi-delict, is found in Roman Law. This category comprised instances of strict liability, that is liability without fault. In Scots law the term quasi-delict has been used to denote delicts in which intention need not be proved, broadly this means that liability in negligence is quasi-delictual rather than delictual. However this use of the term has been criticised and it has been argued that the term quasi-delict should be used only where liability is strict. It is probably true to say that the issue of quasi-delict is ignored for most purposes in the modern context although it may be of academic or historical interest. Readers of this book need not concern themselves with quasi-delict.

An obligation has been defined as "a legal tie by which we may be necessitated or constrained to pay or perform something" (Stair, *Institute*, III, 1). It must be noted that an obligation may be negative so persons may be obliged to refrain from acting. A negative obligation of this nature may be imposed by the court in the form of interdict, an important remedy in some areas of delict. Equally a person's acts or omissions may give rise to a positive obligation, to make reparation, that is to pay damages.

DAMNUM INJURIA DATUM

While contract is concerned with agreements, delict is concerned with wrongs. The obligation to make reparation only arises where three elements are present. There must be *damnum injuria datum,* that is loss caused by a wrong. This approach to delictual liability is a feature of civilian legal systems and derives from the Lex Aquilia of c. 287BC.

Loss may be easily understood in terms of, for example, damage to property, personal injury, interference with physical integrity, affront, interference with the comfortable enjoyment of property or financial loss. However, not all losses are reparable. For example, the law of delict recognises no right to privacy so loss in the form of an invasion of privacy is not reparable. It is best to think of loss in terms of the invasion of a legally protected interest. Different areas of delict protect the citizen in respect of different interests, so for example a person's honour and reputation is protected by the law of defamation while the right to comfortable enjoyment of property free from material harm or substantial inconvenience is protected by the law of nuisance. While most delicts operate within a restricted sphere, you would not raise an action in assault if you had been defamed for instance, the scope of negligence is much broader. As Lord MacMillan stated in *Donoghue v. Stevenson,* "the categories of negligence are never closed". Thus while it is clear that the law of negligence can be mobilised in respect of personal injury or property damage caused through carelessness negligence is not restricted to such forms of loss and has indeed been applied where the harm suffered has been to reputation.

The loss incurred by the pursuer must have been caused by a wrong. A sufficient link between the wrongful act or omission complained of and the resultant harm or loss must be established. Causation is discussed in the chapter on negligence. However it should be noted that causation is relevant in all areas of delict.

An act may be wrongful in itself, such as an assault which is both a crime and a civil wrong. Equally an act that is not in itself wrongful may become wrongful because it invades an interest that is protected by law. So for example while burning refuse in my garden is not wrongful in the absence of local regulations on the emission of smoke, my act may become wrongful if the disturbance and inconvenience caused to neighbours is sufficiently grave to amount in law to a nuisance. Most negligence actions arise from people doing things that they are perfectly entitled to do. However, where there is a risk that actions will harm others, care must be taken so that harm does not materialise. In negligence legal wrongs arise where insufficient care is taken in circumstances where the law imposes a duty to take care and harm results.

The general rule of the common law is that no liability can arise in the absence of *culpa. Culpa* means fault and may be divided into intention on one hand and negligence on the other. Intentional liability arises in respect of deliberate acts done in the knowledge that harm will result whereas negligence consists in exercising insufficient care in circumstances where there is a risk that harm will result if sufficient care is not taken. The most recent authoritative statement divides *culpa* into five categories. This is discussed in the chapter on nuisance. *Culpa* is not peculiar to nuisance, although it is in the context of nuisance that modern discussion on the meaning of *culpa* tends to arise. The requirement of *culpa* is general across the common law of delict although in defamation *culpa* is established by means of a legal fiction.

DELICT AND TORT

Delict in Scotland plays the role fulfilled in England by the law of torts. It must be noted that delict and tort are of ancient origin and developed independently from very different conceptual bases, delict being considerably more influenced by the Roman tradition. There has been considerable cross-fertilisation between delict and tort, but this process did not start until well after the Union of 1707 and is really a phenomenon of the nineteenth and twentieth centuries. The process continues.

Many things that are true of tort apply equally to delict. Many Scots cases have been accepted in England. Conversely many English authorities have been explicitly adopted in Scots law, many have been found acceptable without any need to agonise over the point while there are others that should have been turned back at the border.

There are areas of delict that are distinctly Scottish such as use of land *in aemulationem vicini*. Equally there are delicts in which English authorities are accepted on some points and rejected on others, for example in nuisance. There are areas in which the law is effectively the same in so many respects yet occasionally the underlying jurisdictional disparity in outlook surfaces. This is true of negligence and can be seen in *Maloco v. Littlewoods* (1987) and associated cases. The Scots are not concerned to anything like the degree exhibited by the English with the distinction between misfeasance and non feasance, that is between wrongful acts and omissions.

There are certain areas of modern development such as the economic delicts in which future developments in both jurisdictions are likely to be harmonious. In other areas, such as nuisance, there is scope for distinctively Scottish elements to emerge and become more widely appreciated. In general it is probably true to say that the points of convergence and divergence between delict and tort are less well settled, understood or appreciated than is the case with the Scottish and English law of contract or property.

---

2. NEGLIGENCE: GENERAL

INTERESTS PROTECTED BY THE LAW OF NEGLIGENCE

Actions in negligence arise where harm is caused carelessly or through inadvertence. Negligence is not the appropriate basis for litigation where harm is caused intentionally or deliberately. Where harm is a virtually certain consequence of conduct, then conduct is said to be intentional. This is a different form of *culpa* from negligence. Essentially, negligence arises where there is a **risk** that conduct will cause harm. The existence of a risk suggests that care will be required in conducting the activity, to ensure that the risk does not materialise. The law imposes a duty of care in respect of some risks, but not others depending upon whether the harm to which the risk gives rise constitutes the invasion of an interest that is protected by the law of negligence.

Not all harm caused carelessly is actionable as negligence. It is not every form of harm that gives rise to a legal right to reparation. Different aspects of the law of delict protect different interests. The interests protected by the law of negligence are primarily: physical harm to person and property. Psychiatric health is now recognised as a protected interest so psychiatric harm is in principle, reparable. Liability in negligence for psychiatric harm will be considered separately in a later chapter. In general, financial interests are protected, not by the law of negligence, but by the law of contract. Where financial loss is caused by fraud or by one of the economic delicts, such as passing off, a case in reparation may lie. However, in cases of this nature the wrongful behaviour giving rise to the loss is characterised as intentional rather than negligent, so any claim would not be based on negligence. Unless financial loss is consequential on harm to person or property, in general, the law of negligence provides no remedy. There are, of course, exceptions and these too are considered in a later chapter.

Therefore, when one is considering whether an action in negligence might lie, it is vital to consider the nature of the harm. Physical harm to person or property may give rise to a claim in negligence. Psychiatric harm may also give rise to such a claim. Purely financial harm does not give rise to a negligence claim unless the circumstances fall within one of the recognised exceptions.

ESSENTIAL STEPS IN ESTABLISHING NEGLIGENCE

It is not every careless or inadvertent act that gives rise to a negligence action. Not every risk must be guarded against. Actionable negligence only arises where the loss to the pursuer arises from a **breach** of a **duty of care** owed to the pursuer by the defender. Thus, it must be established that the defender owed the pursuer a duty of care.

If it can be established that the defender did owe the pursuer a duty of care, the next step is to show that the defender breached that duty. In order to do this the abstract concept of duty must be given content. This is achieved by defining the appropriate **standard of care**. The standard of care determines what the defender ought or ought not to have done in the circumstances. The defender's acts or omissions must be measured against the standard of care. If it can be shown that the defender did not take the degree of care required, then it can be held that they breached their duty.

The next step is to show that the harm complained of arose as a result of the defender's breach of duty. In other words, it is necessary to establish **causation**. Even though it can be established that a defender owed a duty of care to the pursuer and that that duty was breached, unless the loss can be directly attributed to that breach, the defender will not be liable in reparation.

Finally, the law will not compensate every loss that arises from a breach of duty. The direct and immediate losses arising from a breach are reparable. Indirect or consequential results of a breach may not be. Losses that are too remote will not be compensated. Thus the rules on **remoteness of damage** have to be considered.

These points will be considered in turn in greater detail. However, you have already learned something useful. Whenever you consider a possible action in negligence, cover the fundamental points in turn. Once you have determined that particular circumstances may give rise to a negligence claim, because harm was caused unintentionally and because the nature of the harm suffered represents the invasion of an interest protected by the law of negligence, the subsequent steps in analysis are always the same. Consider in order the following: was a duty of care owed? If so, was that duty breached? (To answer this you must refer to the standard of care.) Was the harm caused by the breach and finally, are all of the losses suffered reparable or are some or all of them too remote?

This is a logical approach to solving negligence problems which accords with legal theory. However, you will not always find the same sequential approach taken in the case reports. There are various reasons for this; for example, it is not in every case that equal weight will be given to the consideration of all these issues. Nevertheless, a structured approach to solving negligence problems will serve you well in the exam hall.

THE DUTY OF CARE

Duties of care are imposed by law. In some circumstances the duty is imposed by statute. For example, the duty on employers to provide a safe system of work is imposed by the Health and Safety at Work Act 1974, s.2(1). The duty on occupiers of premises to take reasonable care to ensure that premises are safe is imposed by the Occupiers' Liability (Scotland) Act 1960, s.2(1). In the absence of legislation the common law may impose a duty. As a matter of policy the courts limit the number of potential claimants by recognising the existence of a duty of care in some circumstances while denying a duty in others. Thus the duty of care is used as a "threshold device" to limit the field of potential liability.

You need to be able to work out whether, in a given situation, the common law would impose a duty of care. In consideration of this point it is necessary to discuss in outline the development of the modern law of negligence.

Development

The culmination of early developments in the modern law of negligence is found in the celebrated case of *Donoghue v. Stevenson* (1932). Poor Mrs Donoghue allegedly suffered severe gastro-enteritis after a decomposing snail emerged from an opaque bottle of fizzy drink that she was pouring over her ice cream. This may have been ginger beer. Equally, the term "ginger" may have arisen in the generic sense in which it is still used in the West of Scotland. Mrs Donoghue's stomach complaint arose from the fact she had already consumed some of the contents of the bottle.

Mrs Donoghue had no right of action in contract since she had no contract with the manufacturer. Moreover, she had no contract with the cafe owner since the drink had been bought for her by her friend. The House of Lords determined that she had a relevant claim in delict. In a famous passage, Lord Atkin formulated what has become known as the neighbourhood principle.

> "You must take reasonable care to avoid acts or omissions which you can reasonably foresee would be likely to injure your neighbour. Who, then, in law, is my neighbour? The answer seems to be—persons who are so closely and directly affected by my act that I ought reasonably to have them in contemplation when I am directing my mind to the acts or omissions which are called into question."

The case of *Donoghue v. Stevenson* was of tremendous significance. While it was, at the time, possible in both Scottish and English jurisdictions to describe negligence in terms of breach of duty, in English law in particular the courts were reluctant to impose duties in novel circumstances. In short, English courts would only recognise a duty where there was a direct precedent for doing so. This rendered the law inflexible and hampered development. In *Donoghue* Lord Atkin explicitly sought to lay down a general principle of law, the application of which would determine the existence or otherwise of a duty of care whenever loss was caused unintentionally. As Lord MacMillan, one of two Scottish judges on the bench in *Donoghue*, observed: "The categories of negligence are never closed."

The neighbourhood principle in *Donoghue* sets out criteria for determining whether a duty is owed based on foreseeability of harm. If I am going to do something and I can reasonably contemplate that my actions will have a direct effect on you or your property, then I owe you a duty to take care in how I conduct my activities so that I do not cause you harm. If I can, or ought to foresee that my activities might harm you, then I owe you a duty. I should not conduct my activities in disregard of your interests.

Through the application of this simple principle courts were able to hold that duties were owed in a variety of new situations. Indeed, courts expanded the parameters of liability in negligence into new areas in which liability in negligence would not, traditionally, have arisen. The best examples of such ground-breaking decisions are: *Dorset Yacht Co v. Home Office* (1970) and *Hedley Byrne v. Heller and Partners* (1964).

In the former case the House of Lords found that prison officers owed a duty of care to the owners of a yacht damaged when borstal boys under their control sought to escape from an island in Poole harbour. This decision was remarkable since one cannot normally be held liable for the acts of independent third parties. Critical to the decision was the view that the prison officers had a supervisory role over the boys and ought to have foreseen an escape attempt. Some of the boys had a record of absconding. Since the officers knew of the presence of the yacht, and that the yacht offered the only feasible means of escape, they should have foreseen the events that transpired. The boys escaped, commandeered the yacht and crashed it. The officers owed a duty of care to the owners of the yacht since they ought to have foreseen harm to their property as the result of the negligent way in which they exercised their supervisory role. They had gone to bed and left the boys to their own devices.

In *Hedley Byrne* the House of Lords held that a duty of care could be owed when a reference was given regarding the financial position of a merchant bankers' client. This was so, even though the loss complained of was purely financial. The party who had sought the reference was an advertising agency that went ahead on the strength of the reference, placing adverts on behalf of the client. In so doing they incurred substantial debts which the client was unable to pay. Because financial loss to the party relying on the statement was foreseeable it was held that the merchant bankers owed a duty of care. In the event *Hedley Byrne* were not liable in damages, because they had given the reference with an explicit disclaimer of responsibility.

However, there have been many instances in which courts were reluctant to hold that a duty of care existed notwithstanding the reasonable foreseeability of harm to pursuers. It became clear that decisions could be influenced by considerations of policy. Sometimes such considerations were made explicit. For example in cases involving psychiatric harm the argument was advanced that recognition of a duty of care would "open the floodgates" to spurious claims. On other occasions, policy considerations were present, but not made explicit.

The flexible approach to liability in negligence instigated by *Donoghue* with foreseeability of harm as the governing criterion, reached its zenith in the House of Lords case of *Anns v. Merton Borough Council* (1978). Lord Wilberforce proposed a two-part test:

> "First one has to ask whether, as between the alleged wrongdoer and the person who has suffered damage there is a sufficient relationship of proximity or neighbourhood such that, in the reasonable contemplation of the former, carelessness on his part may be likely to cause damage to the latter, in which case a prima facie duty of care arises. Secondly, if the first question is answered affirmatively, it is necessary to consider whether there are any considerations which ought to negative, or reduce or limit the scope of the duty or the persons to whom it is owed or the damages to which a breach of it may give rise...."

Had the approach suggested by Lord Wilberforce found favour it would have meant prima facie liability in negligence based firmly on the application of the neighbourhood principle. Liability would then have been confirmed or denied following further considerations such as the nature of the loss or policy. However, this approach to liability in negligence was not well received.

While Lord Atkin expressly sought to liberalise the law of negligence there have always been those who felt that he stated the basis for liability too broadly. The effect of the Wilberforce doctrine in *Anns* would have been further liberalisation. This was out of step with the tendency of the courts at the time to rein in negligence, that is to restrict rather than continue to expand the scope of negligence.

The two-stage approach outlined in *Anns* was not well received and courts departed from it in subsequent cases. Ultimately *Anns* was over-ruled by the House of Lords in *Murphy v. Brentwood DC* (1991).

Both *Anns* and *Murphy* are cases involving pure economic loss which is considered more fully in the next chapter. The period since *Anns* is one in which courts have shown great reluctance to expand liability in negligence by way of recognising a duty of care in novel situations. The current period is one in which courts tend to restrict rather than expand the scope of liability. This phenomenon, and in particular the process whereby Lord Wilberforce's two-stage test was rejected, has been aptly described as the "retreat from *Anns*".

The current situation does not quite return us to the English position pre-*Donoghue* where no duty arose unless there was a precedent for recognising one, since there are criteria according to which a duty may be recognised. Moreover, a substantial body of precedent has developed since *Donoghue* in which duties of care have been recognised and of course, if a new case falls within the facts of a previous case, then whether or not a duty is imposed will depend upon precedent.

It is important to note therefore that in novel situations, that is, where there is no sufficiently analogous precedent for imposing a duty of care, the *Donoghue* approach has been superseded.

In novel situations no duty will be recognised unless three requirements are satisfied. First, harm to the pursuer must be reasonably foreseeable. Secondly, there must be a close degree of proximity between the parties. Thirdly, it must be fair just and reasonable to impose a duty. This tripartite test arises from *Caparo v. Dickman* (1990). It appears that Scottish Courts will adopt this approach in novel cases even where the harm complained of is physical damage to person or property. This was the approach taken in an Outer House case that involved personal injury, *Gibson v. Orr* (1999). Finally, it is recognised that policy considerations may influence the decisions of the courts.

ESTABLISHING THE DUTY OF CARE: TO WHOM IS A DUTY OWED?

A duty of care is not owed to the whole world. It is not enough for liability to say that a reasonable person ought to have contemplated that their negligent conduct could have harmed somebody. The pursuer in particular has to be someone whom the defender ought to have contemplated, otherwise there is no duty. The field of potential pursuers is limited by the requirement of proximity.

So in the first case of nervous shock to be considered by the House of Lords, *Bourhill v. Young* (1942), it was held that no duty was owed by the defender to the pursuer. The defender drove a motorcycle negligently past the inside of a parked tram at a road junction. He collided with a car that was turning right and was killed. The pursuer, a pregnant fishwife, was collecting her creel from the far side of the tram. She did not see the collision, but heard it. She later saw blood on the road when she returned after delivering her fish. She attributed her subsequent miscarriage to nervous shock sustained at the scene of the accident. Her action failed for lack of proximity. While there was no doubt that pedestrians and other road users were within the reasonable contemplation of the deceased, Mrs Bourhill herself was outwith the area within which a duty of care was owed. The motorcyclist could not reasonably foresee that he would injure Mrs Bourhill.

Similarly in *Hill v. Chief Constable of West Yorkshire* (1989) the mother of the final victim of Peter Sutcliffe, the Yorkshire Ripper, sued in negligence. It was alleged that the police were negligent in failing to identify and apprehend Sutcliffe prior to the murder of Jacqueline Hill. Indeed, it was admitted by the police that they had made mistakes during the process of investigation. The case was unsuccessful. While it was reasonably foreseeable that young women in general in the Leeds area were in danger while the Ripper remained at large, no duty of care was owed to Jacqueline Hill in particular. This case also involved a policy consideration. It was felt that the admission of an actionable duty of care in such circumstances would have a detrimental effect on the conduct of police operations.

In essence the requirement of proximity means that there has to be some link established between pursuer and defender. If there is no such link, there will be no duty. The requirement of proximity effectively narrows the scope of the neighbourhood principle.

ESTABLISHING BREACH OF DUTY: THE STANDARD OF CARE

Establishing a duty of care is only the first step in an action based on negligence. Next it has to be established that the duty was breached. This raises the issue, how much care was the defender obliged to exercise? The defender will only be liable to make reparation if it can be shown that the care taken was less than that required by law. In other words the defender's conduct must have fallen short of that necessary to fulfil the duty. The abstract concept of duty of care is given content by the standard of care. It is up to pursuers to stipulate exactly what the duty was, what the defender should have or should not have done, and to specify the way in which their conduct deviated from the standard required.

The standard of care imposed by law is that of the reasonable man, or ordinarily careful person. So a defender will only be liable if his or her conduct showed less care than would have been exercised by a reasonable person in the position of the defender at the time at which the event occurred. The standard of the reasonable man is an objective standard and courts will not enquire too deeply into the idiosyncrasies of the individual. Thus a learner driver owes the same standard of care to other road users as an experienced driver (*Nettleship v. Weston* (1971)). If this seems harsh on the learner driver, the point is that other road users and pedestrians are entitled to expect a certain degree of care, not differing standards according to the experience or lack of it of the driver.

It is important to note that the standard of care is a flexible concept. The degree of care required by law varies according to the circumstances. Some activities require a level of care that is little more than mundane, for example, applying the handbrake when parking a car. Other activities require the most elaborate precautions, open-heart surgery or nuclear fusion for example.

The point was put well by Lord Neaves in *Chalmers v. Dixon* (1876): "No prudent man in carrying a lighted candle through a powder magazine would fail to take more care than if he was going through a damp cellar." As Lord MacMillan stated in *Muir v. Glasgow Corporation* (1955): "There is no absolute standard, but it may be said generally that the degree of care required varies directly with the risk involved."

ESTABLISHING BREACH OF DUTY: THE CALCULUS OF RISK

Ultimately, courts will determine what precautions a reasonable person in the defender's position ought to take or the level of care that ought to be exercised. This determination has been assisted by the identification of factors that ought to be taken into consideration in assessing risk. The most relevant considerations are the likelihood of the risk of harm materialising and the magnitude of the harm if the risk does materialise. This aspect of the law of negligence may be explained most clearly in the context of accidents at work.

It has been held that there is a duty on employers to weigh on the one hand, the magnitude of risk, the likelihood of an accident happening and the possible gravity of any accident against, on the other hand, the difficulty, expense and disadvantage of taking any particular precaution. This balancing process is termed "the calculus of risk". While these factors derive from the judgement of Lord Reid in *Morris v. West Hartlepool Steam Navigation Co Ltd* (1956) and are commonly illustrated by reference to other employment cases, the basic approach of weighing up the risks against the practicability of precautions is not restricted to the employment field.

In *Brisco v. Secretary of State for Scotland* (1997) a prison officer sought damages of £2,000 in respect of a broken bone in his little toe, sustained when a heavy fence post thrown from above landed on him during a simulated riot. The pursuer contended that his employers were in breach of their duty to him in failing to issue an instruction forbidding the throwing of heavy objects. In the Inner House the factors outlined in the previous paragraph were considered. In the light of the need for riot training of prison officers under realistic circumstances the instruction contended for by the pursuer would have amounted to a disadvantage. This disadvantage was sufficient to outweigh the relatively slight risk involved. Accordingly there was no breach of duty.

In *Latimer v. AEC Ltd* (1953) a factory floor became slippery after flooding. Three tons of sawdust was put down on the floor, but the plaintiff slipped on an uncovered part of the floor and was injured. He argued that the factory should have been closed down. The House of Lords held that the employer had done all that a reasonable employer would have done. Closing down the factory would have meant a loss of production and the expense and disadvantage of this was not outweighed by the relatively small danger to which the plaintiff had been exposed.

A further means of contending for a particular standard of care is to show that defenders have not followed usual practice. The House of Lords decision in *Brown v. Rolls Royce* (1960) demonstrates that failure to adopt a normal practice is not conclusive proof of negligence, but merely a fact from which negligence may be inferred. The plaintiff contracted dermatitis. He was a machine oiler whose hands were constantly in contact with oil. Evidence was led to show that it was common practice for employers to provide Rozalex #1, a barrier cream. Rolls Royce had not done so, but they had sought medical advice on the issue and contended that Rozalex was not an effective prophylactic. They had made alternative provision in the form of adequate washing facilities. Rolls Royce was not in breach. They had not neglected to take precautions, but had considered the issue, made provision and had demonstrated the conduct and judgement of a reasonable employer. Thus, normal practice may be of evidential value, but will not, in itself, determine the issue.

ESTABLISHING BREACH OF DUTY: LIKELIHOOD OF INJURY

The duty of care involves the requirement to guard against risks that are likely to materialise, but not against all eventualities. One is only liable for consequences that a reasonable person in the position of the defender would have contemplated in the circumstances when they occurred.

As Lord Oaksey explained: "The standard of care in the law of negligence is the standard of an ordinary careful man, but in my opinion an ordinary careful man does not take precautions against every foreseeable risk. He can, of course, foresee the possibility of many risks, but life would be almost impossible if he were to attempt to take precautions against every risk which he can foresee. He takes precautions against risks which are reasonably likely to happen. Many foreseeable risks are extremely unlikely to happen and cannot be guarded against except by almost complete isolation".

The context for these remarks was the English House of Lords case of *Bolton v. Stone* (1951). In that case a cricket ball was struck right out of a cricket ground where it injured a person around one hundred yards from the wicket. While the event was foreseeable, balls had been struck out of the ground six times in the previous 30 years, the defendants who operated the cricket ground were not obliged to have guarded against it. The risk of injury was so remote that a reasonable person would not have anticipated it.

A similar issue was determined by the House of Lords in the earlier Scottish case of *Muir v. Glasgow Corporation* (1943). Participants in a Sunday school picnic in King's Park, Glasgow sought shelter from the rain in a tea-room run by the Corporation. The Corporation's employee on the premises, Mrs Alexander, gave permission for the picnic and allowed an urn full of boiling water to be carried down a passageway to the tea-room. The urn was dropped in the passageway scalding several children who were queuing to buy sweeties. The Corporation was sued in negligence.

While it was held that Mrs Alexander owed a duty of care to the children she was not in breach of that duty. The spillage was not foreseeable as a reasonable and probable consequence of her conduct in allowing the urn to be carried. She was entitled to assume that the carriers would have been reasonably careful. With the benefit of hindsight we can see that spillage was a possibility, but the Court deemed that Mrs Alexander would not have foreseen the event as a possibility let alone a probability.

The extent of liability is limited by taking a practical approach. Foreseeability is relevant not only to establishing the existence of a duty, but also to determining whether the defender's conduct constitutes a breach. *Bolton v. Stone* illustrates the point that foreseeability of harm is a necessary, but not a sufficient requirement for breach of duty. For a duty to be breached the conduct complained of must have as its reasonable and probable consequence harm to the pursuer.

Bolton v. Stone may be contrasted with the case of *Lamond v. Glasgow Corporation* (1968) in which a golf ball was hit onto a footpath where it struck the pursuer on the head. In that case the duty of care was breached since the event was not only possible, but also probable. It was established in evidence that on average six thousand golf balls were played onto the footpath every year although there was no previously reported instance of anybody having been struck.

The House of Lords decision in *Hughes v. Lord Advocate* (1963) demonstrates a very important point. Although the precise way in which an accident occurs may not be reasonably foreseeable, if some accident of that type or general nature is foreseeable then liability may be established. This case involved a hole in the road, covered with a tent, but otherwise insufficiently guarded. Boys investigated with a paraffin lamp that had been marking the road works. The lamp was knocked down the hole. This ignited gas and caused an explosion that burned one of the boys badly. It was held that the explosion was not foreseeable. However it was foreseeable that a child might enter the tent with a lamp, that paraffin might spill and that the child might be burned. Therefore the duty of care owed to pedestrians was breached.

Similarly in *Wilson v. Chief Constable of Lothian and Borders Police* (1999) a man died of hypothermia having been released by police in a drunken condition in an isolated place at 5.45 on a January morning. It had been snowing heavily, the temperature was 0 degrees. The body was found a week later 2.2 miles from the site of release. It was held that the police were not bound to have foreseen the man's death from hypothermia, but they should have foreseen that he would be exposed to various risks of severe harm. They were under a particular duty to have regard to the reasonably foreseeable consequences of his release. The officers concerned had failed to direct their minds to the likely consequences of their act and had exposed the deceased to unnecessary risk. The chain of events that was foreseeable was not different in kind from those that led to his death.

ESTABLISHING BREACH OF DUTY: SUMMARY

In summary, once the existence of a duty of care is established the onus is on the pursuer to establish that the duty has been breached. In pleadings the pursuer must aver the standard of care applicable. The pursuer will argue that the defender exercised less care than was called for in the circumstances, that is that the defender's acts or omissions fell short of the appropriate standard. The degree of care that ought to be exercised will vary according to the nature of the activity that gave rise to the harm. Activities that are inherently hazardous require more care than activities where the risk to others is slight.

Liability arises only in respect of events that are the reasonable and probable consequence of the breach. The precise details of the harmful incident do not have to be foreseeable so long as an event of that nature or type ought to have been foreseen.

CAUSATION

It is necessary to show that the harm complained of resulted from the defender's breach. A causal link must be established. It must be shown by the pursuer that "but for" the breach, the loss would not have occurred. Thus in *McWilliams v. Sir Archibald Arrol & Co* (1962), employers were in breach of their duty since they failed to provide a steel erector with a safety belt. However, they were not liable when he plunged to his death since it was established in evidence that even if he had been given a belt, the steel erector would not have worn it. Similarly in *Barnett v. Chelsea and Kensington Hospital Management Committee* (1969) the casualty officer was in breach of duty in failing to see a patient who presented with violent vomiting. The patient died later of arsenic poisoning. The hospital was not liable despite the breach, because it was established that the patient would have died anyway. His death was not attributable to the doctor's breach of duty.

So the breach must be the factual cause of the loss. This is expressed as the *causa sine qua non*. This is a necessary, but not sufficient basis for establishing causation. In order to establish causation it is also necessary to establish that the breach is the *causa causans*. That is, the breach must be the legal cause in the sense of being the effective, dominant or immediate cause. Of course, in many circumstances the factual and legal cause are the same, the issue only arises where there are complications in the causal chain. Such complications arise, for example, where there are further acts by the pursuer or by third parties which have some effect on the victim.

The difficulties associated with causation have been exercising the minds of lawyers for a rather long time. This is illustrated by the following passage from Roman Law that will enable the distinction between *causa sine qua non* and *causa causans* to be illustrated.

> "Celsus writes that if one attacker inflicts a mortal wound on a slave and another person later finishes him off, he who struck the earlier blow will not be liable for a killing, but for wounding, because he actually perished as a result of another wound". (D.9.2.11.3.)

The original wound is a *causa sine qua non*, since "but for" the wound the slave might not have been lying around in a position where he could be wounded again. So the original wound is the factual cause. However, the original wound is not the *causa causans*. The *causa causans* is the second attack that kills the slave. The second attack is the effective, dominant or immediate cause of death. The second attack is a *novus actus interveniens* (new act intervening) which breaks the chain of causation between the infliction of the original wound and death, relieving the original wrongdoer from liability.

In *McKew v. Holland & Hannen & Cubitts (Scotland) Ltd* (1969) the pursuer injured his ankle as a result of the defenders' negligence. His leg thereafter was liable to "give way" on occasions. After the accident he went to visit a flat. Access to the flat was by way of a stair with no handrail. The pursuer descended the stairway without care, his leg gave way, he panicked and jumped down 10 steps causing further injury to his leg. The court held the defenders liable for the original injury, but not the second. By descending the stairs without care the pursuer's own act constituted a *novus actus interveniens*. The defenders' breach was a *causa sine qua non* of the second injury, but it was not the *causa causans*.

A further complicating factor arises where there may be more than one cause for the harm suffered. In *Wardlaw v. Bonnington Castings Ltd* (1956) the pursuer contracted pneumoconiosis from breathing in dust at work. The dust might have come from the hammer that he operated for which there was no known means of providing protection and therefore no breach of duty on the part of the employers. Equally the dust might have come from grinders and other machinery for which protection could have been, but was not provided. Accordingly employers were not in breach in respect of one possible source, but were in breach in respect of the other. The House of Lords held that the pursuer could succeed in negligence if he could show that dust from the source for which the defenders were in breach had materially contributed to his injuries.

This point was extended further in the subsequent House of Lords case of *McGhee v. National Coal Board* (1972). In that case also there were two possible sources of harm, one of which involved breach of duty and the other did not. Again it was impossible to determine which source was the effective cause of the pursuer's dermatitis. It was held that the pursuer could succeed if he could show that the source in respect of which the defenders were in breach materially contributed to the risk of injury. Where there are a number of potential sources of harm the issue of causation is difficult and the decision in *McGhee* in particular may be regarded as controversial.

REMOTENESS

Where loss occurs there may be no end to the consequences. Imagine I am knocked off my motorbike by the negligence of a car driver while on my way to a job interview. I can seek reparation in respect of my physical injuries both in terms of pain and suffering and any disability I sustain. But my loss does not end there. Because I am in hospital when I was scheduled to be at the interview I do not get the new job, I have to continue in my present job that pays far less. My family suffers financially and eventually my marriage breaks down due to financial strains. Such losses would be regarded as too speculative to be reparable. After all, I may have failed the interview.

A line has to be drawn somewhere between consequences which the negligent defender must bear and those which must be borne by the victim. Thus we have the concept of remoteness of damage. The law will not compensate damage that is too remote.

The difficulty is in determining the criteria that courts apply to determine whether loss is too remote. There are two approaches. One is that defenders are liable for the direct consequences of their acts. The problem with this view is the lack of criteria for distinguishing the direct and the indirect. The other approach is to hold defenders liable only for the reasonably foreseeable consequences of their acts.

The former approach is associated with *Re Polemis v. Furniss Withy & Co Ltd* (1921). In that case a ship carrying a cargo of, *inter alia*, petrol was berthed at Casablanca. Dockers working on the ship dropped a plank into the hold. There was a spark and this ignited petrol vapour. There was an explosion and a fire. The Court of Appeal unequivocally rejected foreseeability as the test in that case. The harm was the direct result of the defendant's negligence and full damages were awarded.

The latter approach is associated with *Overseas Tankship (UK) Ltd v. Morts Dock and Engineering Co Ltd (The Wagon Mound No. 1)* (1961). Heavy furnace oil, not easily combustible, was negligently spilt from a ship in Sydney harbour. Workmen were using welding equipment on the wharf and molten metal fell into the harbour. This ignited either cotton waste floating on the oil or the wooden structure of the wharf that in turn ignited the cotton waste. The oil was set ablaze and there was an enormous fire that destroyed the wharf and some surrounding buildings. The Privy Council rejected the *Polemis* approach holding that in order to be recoverable, the damage had to be a reasonably foreseeable consequence of the defendant's negligence. The defendants could not have foreseen the fire arising in this way. Accordingly, they were not liable.

The authorities are of little assistance in determining which of these two approaches is favoured in Scots law. Elements of either approach may be found in cases both before and after *Polemis* and *The Wagon Mound*. It is common to cite Lord Kinloch's dictum in *Allan v. Barclay* (1864).

"The grand rule on the subject of damages is that none can be claimed except such as naturally and directly arise out of the wrong done; and such therefore, as may reasonably be supposed to have been in the view of the wrongdoer."

The problem here is that this dictum embraces both approaches assuming that the second part of the sentence is read to mean what is reasonably foreseeable. Natural and direct consequences are equated with consequences that are foreseeable. We know from *Polemis* and *The Wagon Mound* that the two may be distinguished. In most instances, either approach will normally produce the same result. This may explain why the issue has never been fully resolved. It has been argued that Scottish courts combine both approaches, drawing the line somewhere before losses are deemed too speculative.

THE THIN SKULL RULE.

The "thin skull" rule may be seen as a limitation on the rules on remoteness. Just as in criminal law, one takes one's victim as one finds him. So if I negligently injure a person who turns out to be a haemophiliac and bleeds to death in circumstances where a normally healthy person would only suffer a broken limb, then I am fully liable for causing death. However, physical harm must be a foreseeable and probable consequence of my conduct. The rule only operates after breach of duty is established. If there is a duty to avoid causing physical harm and that harm results the thin skull rule operates to allow recovery in respect of the unforeseeable extent of the loss. An example of such a case is *McKillen v. Barclay Curle* (1967) in which a negligently inflicted fractured rib caused a reactivation of the pursuer's tuberculosis.

LIABILITY FOR THE ACTS OF THIRD PARTIES

Outwith circumstances in which vicarious liability operates, one is in general not liable for the deliberate acts of third parties. Normally any such act would constitute a *novus actus interveniens* breaking the chain of causation between the defender's breach and the pursuer's loss. Liability in negligence in such circumstances is very much the exception rather than the rule.

The classic case is *Dorset Yacht Co v. Home Office* (1970). This case has already been discussed. Liability for the acts of thirds parties has also been considered in the context of whether there is a duty owed to neighbours in respect of damage caused by persons entering the pursuer's property. In 1986 the case of *Squires v. Perth & Kinross District Council* (1986) was determined in the Inner House. The second defenders, a firm of building contractors, were found liable in negligence having breached a duty of care owed to the pursuers to secure premises against access by third parties. The builders had been carrying out renovation work on flats above the pursuers' premises, a jewellers shop. A thief had gained access to one of the flats which was not properly secured and had broken through the floor into the shop below.

The Court held that this was an event that ought to have been foreseen and guarded against. As Lord Wheatley said: "Any reasonable person in occupancy and control would have foreseen the likelihood of what in fact occurred."

The following year the case of *Maloco v. Littlewoods* (1987) (also reported *sub nom Smith v. Littlewoods*) was decided in the House of Lords. The defenders owned an empty cinema, the Regal in Dunfermline. Children broke in and started fires which damaged neighbouring property. The House of Lords held that there was no breach of any duty owed to neighbouring proprietors.

Lord McKay, a Scottish judge, appeared to determine the case on the ground that the event that transpired was not foreseeable. The defenders did not know of previous acts of vandalism involving fire. Since the cinema was not an obvious fire risk the defenders were not under a duty to anticipate the possibility of fire by vandals.

However, the decision in *Maloco* may be better explained as following the English Court of Appeal case of *Perl Exporters v. Camden LBC* (1984). In that case the defendants were held to owe no duty to neighbours to secure their property, despite the fact that they had been made well aware of the accessibility of the property to vagrants and of the concerns of the plaintiffs regarding security. When thieves broke through the adjoining wall and stole garments belonging to the plaintiffs, Perl sued in negligence. Notwithstanding the manifest carelessness of the defendants it was held that no duty of care was owed.

Lord Goff stated: "Is every occupier of a terraced house under a duty to his neighbours to shut his windows or lock his door when he goes out, or to keep access to his cellars secure, or even to remove his fire escape, at the risk of being held liable in damages if thieves thereby obtain access to his own house and thence to his neighbour's house? I cannot think that the law imposes any such duty."

The point is that English law demonstrates great reluctance to recognise a duty of care in respect of a pure omission. English law imposes no duty on proprietors to secure their property against third parties even though it is foreseeable that such persons may use their access to the property to cause harm to neighbouring properties. In *Perl* and *Maloco* it was not any positive act on the part of the defending parties that was complained of, but a failure to act in circumstances where the law recognises no duty to act.

Since *Maloco* is a decision of the House of Lords in a Scottish case there is little scope for doubting that this is also the law of Scotland. This means that if *Squires*, or a similar case fell to be decided in the future, it is most likely that a court would reach the opposite conclusion. The fact that harm is foreseeable is beside the point. The point is that the law imposes no duty to secure one's property to protect one's neighbours.

WRONGFUL CONCEPTION

Within the last 20 years there has been a number of actions brought against doctors and their employers in respect of the birth of unplanned or unwanted children. The general tendency has been to admit such claims.

Such a claim may arise from the failure of hospital staff to warn a pregnant mother of potential physical or mental impairment in the foetus so that the mother is denied the opportunity to terminate the pregnancy. It is established that a duty of care to inform the mother is owed in such circumstances. If the duty is breached, damages will be recoverable. The Scots case of *McLelland v. Greater Glasgow Health Board* (2001) follows the earlier decision of the Court of Appeal in *McKay v. Essex Area Health Authority* (1982).

Another way in which such claims arise is where a sterilisation has been performed negligently or, more pertinently, where the patient has been negligently informed that the operation has been a success when it was not. The subsequent birth of a child has been held to be a reparable loss.

While the moral aspects of regarding the birth of a child as a loss provide scope for discussion, the legal point with which we are concerned here is the extent of recovery in damages. This has been ruled upon recently by the House of Lords in the case of *McFarlane v. Tayside Health Board* (1999). In *McFarlane* the male pursuer, a father of four, underwent a vasectomy and was subsequently given the "all clear" whereas in fact the operation had been unsuccessful. Subsequently his wife conceived a fifth child. The McFarlanes sued, seeking solatium in respect of pain, suffering and inconvenience consequential on pregnancy and childbirth and damages in respect of the financial costs of bringing up the child.

At first instance the Lord Ordinary, (Lord Gill) accepted that a duty of care was owed the parents, but refused to countenance either the birth of a healthy child as a reparable loss or pregnancy and childbirth as personal injury. On reclaiming the Second Division reversed this decision. Unplanned conception was held to amount to a loss and the McFarlanes were awarded both solatium and damages in respect of financial costs of upbringing.

The defenders appealed to the House of Lords on the basis that natural processes of conception and childbirth could not in law amount to personal injury. This argument was rejected and the mother's claim for solatium was allowed by a majority (Lord Millet dissenting). However, the claim for financial costs was rejected unanimously. This loss was treated as economic loss. The Court determined that it would not be fair, just and reasonable to impose liability on the defenders in respect of such financial costs. In other words, as it has been put by one commentator, "doctors and the NHS are not to pay for the upbringing of healthy children".

It must be noted that the McFarlanes' child was born free of physical or mental impairment. The case leaves the position of disabled children unclear. Had the child been born with some kind of disability or impairment, associated costs of upbringing might possibly have been recoverable. Lord Steyn reserved opinion on this point.

DEFENCES

In general the pursuer's pleadings may be attacked at any point. In defence it may be argued that: no duty of care was owed the pursuer; the appropriate standard of care was exercised; the alleged harm was not caused by the pursuer; the alleged loss was too remote. Note that the facts averred by the pursuer may also be challenged. The defender may be able to establish in proof a very different version of events. The defender may challenge the extent of harm averred by the pursuer.

Over and above any such attack on fundamental aspects of the pursuer's case, the defender may argue that the pursuer contributed to his or her losses. This is a plea of contributory negligence. In personal injury cases such a plea is more or less routine. It must be established that the pursuer was at fault in that his or her act or omission fell below the standard of a reasonable person in the pursuer's position. A common example is where a passenger in a car is injured as a result of the driver's negligence, but injuries are exacerbated, because the passenger has failed to wear a seatbelt.

The effect of a successful plea of contributory negligence is to reduce the sum payable in damages by an amount to reflect the degree of the pursuer's own contribution to the harm sustained (Law Reform (Contributory Negligence) Act 1945, s.1). Prior to the 1945 Act contributory negligence was a complete defence, exonerating the defender entirely from the obligation to make reparation.

Where contribution is established courts apportion blame for the damage between the parties and seek to effect a reduction in damages that is just and equitable. For example, in *Sayers v. Harlow UDC* (1958) damages were reduced by 25 per cent to reflect the plaintiff's own contribution to her injuries. She had been trapped in a public toilet cubicle, but in attempting to climb out was held to have contributed to her losses. Her foot slipped on the toilet roll holder and she fell to the floor.

In reducing damages courts must determine the total damages that would have been awarded had there been no contribution by the defender. Thus we can see the exact apportionment of blame determined by the court. In *Campbell v. Gillespie* (1996) a mechanic was working at night on a broken down lorry on the A87 between Shiel Bridge and Kyle of Lochalsh. This road is fast in places and it is not lit. The lorry's lights had been disconnected and the mechanic should have provided protection by parking his own, lit vehicle behind the lorry. There was a police warning sign and other vehicles had avoided the lorry before the pursuer's husband ploughed into the back of it at 60 mph or faster in his Vauxhall Astra. The car driver was held 60 per cent to blame, the mechanic, 40 per cent.

A further defence is afforded by the doctrine of *volenti non fit injuria* (to one consenting no wrong is done). *Volenti* operates where it can be held that the pursuer has consented to the risk undertaken by the defender. The defender must establish that the pursuer had knowledge of the risk and willingly assented to it. *Volenti* is a complete defence. Where established it relieves the defender from all liability. The defence of *volenti* does not apply to passengers in road vehicles (Road Traffic Act 1988, s.149). Thus a claim against an over enthusiastic driver who has crashed cannot be defeated by arguing that the passenger should have asked to leave the vehicle when the dangerous nature of the driving first became apparent. Drivers must by law have third party insurance cover. Where there is no such cover the Motor Insurance Bureau will step in and meet established claims. No such restriction applies to aircraft. In *Morris v. Murray* (1991) two friends took off in a light aircraft following an afternoon's heavy drinking. The plane crashed shortly after take off and the injured passenger sued the pilot's estate. The defence of *volenti* was successfully established.

It should be noted that *volenti* is not restricted in scope to negligence actions, but is a generally available defence in delict. For example in the assault case of *Reid v. Mitchell* (1885) it was argued that the pursuer was *volens* of the risk of falling off the haycart. The defence did not succeed since it was held that the pursuer was not a willing participant in the general larking about.

---

3. NEGLIGENCE: RECOVERY OF PURE ECONOMIC LOSS

INTRODUCTION

The recovery of financial or economic loss in negligence poses difficulties. In order to understand what types of economic loss are recoverable it is first necessary to distinguish the different forms such loss may take. Economic loss falls into one of three classifications, derivative, secondary and pure.

Derivative economic loss arises where financial loss follows as a consequence of harm to the person or property of the pursuer. Derivative economic loss is reparable.

Secondary economic loss arises where financial loss follows as a consequence of harm to the person or property of third parties. Secondary economic loss is not reparable.

Pure economic loss arises where the only form of harm suffered is financial and there is no loss in the form of personal injury or property damage. Generally, pure economic loss is not recoverable in negligence. However, there are circumstances in which exceptions are made to the general rule.

Economic wellbeing is not an interest that is protected by the law of negligence. Law does not in general impose a duty of care on persons not to cause others economic loss. In fact causing economic loss to others is an integral feature of a market economy where competition operates. If a successful company gains more customers it does so at the expense of less successful companies. This is not a legal wrong.

The general rule is that actions to recover pure economic loss may not competently be grounded in negligence. However, where pure economic loss is the result, not of negligence, but of deliberate or intentional wrongful conduct, such as fraud, defamation or wrongful interference with contracts, damages may indeed be sought. Moreover, economic loss may be recoverable in contract. Of course, this depends upon the existence of a contract between pursuer and defender. Recovery in the circumstances will depend upon the terms of the contract. In short, purely economic interests are protected by the law of contract and by the intentional delicts, but not, in general, by the law of negligence.

In negligence the distinction between harm to property or person and purely financial harm is viewed as fundamental. This view was challenged in *Anns v. Merton London Borough Council* (1978), but was affirmed afresh by the House of Lords in *Murphy v. Brentwood District Council* (1991) in which *Anns* was over-ruled.

DERIVATIVE ECONOMIC LOSS AND DEFECTIVE PROPERTY

Subject to rules on remoteness financial loss which is a consequence of harm to property or person is recoverable. Thus, if you injure me, you may be liable in damages not only in respect of my pain and suffering, but also for my loss of earnings and relatives' services or costs of nursing.

If you damage my car through your negligence then you must pay for its repair. The financial costs are derivative of harm to my property. However, some care must be taken when considering goods that are defective from the outset. If an electrical appliance has some latent defect that causes my house to burn down, then the cost of rebuilding my house is derivative economic loss and recoverable, since this is an example of defective property damaging other property. Where defective goods cause injury, this is recoverable on the principle of *Donoghue v. Stevenson* (1932). (See also *Grant v. Australian*

Knitting Mills (1936) and the Consumer Protection Act 1987). However, the cost of repairing or replacing defective goods that do not harm either other property or persons is only recoverable in contract.

The same principles that apply to defective goods also apply to defective buildings. A defect that is not dangerous, such as defective plasterwork, does not amount to property damage, but a defect in quality. As such it is regarded as pure economic loss. There may be a remedy in contract, but in circumstances where the pursuer has no contract with the plasterer, for example because the defective work was carried out for a builder by a sub-contractor, recovery will not be possible and the loss will lie where it falls. (*D&F Estates Ltd v. Church Commissioners for England* (1989)).

To be recoverable damage caused by defective property must be damage caused to other, different property. Thus if a house is built on inadequate foundations, consequent damage to walls in the form of cracking and subsidence is not derivative loss, but there is a defect in the quality of the building which amounts to pure economic loss. (*Murphy v. Brentwood District Council*).

SECONDARY ECONOMIC LOSS

The rules on secondary economic loss, like rules on remoteness, serve to draw a line under the liability of defenders. Were this not the case, then defenders could be liable to a degree out of all proportion to the nature of their wrongdoing. Moreover, liability would arise in respect of an indeterminate class of potential litigants. This of course would be completely unacceptable. Thus in *Reavis v. Clan Line Steamers* (1925) the pursuer failed to recover losses arising from the death of members of her orchestra when the ship on which they were travelling sank. The shipping company, whose negligence was responsible for the accident were not liable to her for losses arising from the inability of the deceased to fulfil their contracts with her.

So far as property damage is concerned the leading case is *Dynamco v. Holland, Hannen & Cubitts* (1971). The pursuers lost production in their factory as the result of a power cut. The defenders had negligently severed a power line. Since the power line was the property of the electricity company and not of the pursuers, the pursuers' losses were secondary and thus not recoverable.

An important point to note is that foreseeability of harm to pursuers is not the issue. This is well illustrated by the case of *East Lothian Angling Association v. Haddington Town Council* (1980). In that case the pursuers' economic interests were adversely affected by pollution of a river by the defenders. The pollution affected fishing that in turn affected the sale of permits. It was averred that since the existence of the pursuers was known to the defenders, a duty of care was owed on the basis of the neighbourhood principle. This argument, like a similar argument posed earlier in *Dynamco*, failed. The fact that the pursuers had no proprietary interest in the subjects affected by the negligent act proved fatal to the claim. This defect could not be made good by any attempt to establish proximity between the parties.

PURE ECONOMIC LOSS

While pure economic loss is in general not recoverable in negligence there are exceptions. Exceptions to the general rule on non-recovery in negligence for pure economic loss may be brought together under one head. There is no duty in negligence to avoid causing financial loss save, in the words of Lord Bridge in *Murphy*: "by reason of some special relationship of proximity which imposes on the tortfeasor a duty of care to protect against economic loss".

Therefore, before a duty of care can be held to lie in respect of pure economic loss, the pursuer must satisfy what have been termed enhanced requirements of proximity. In addition, following *Caparo Industries plc v. Dickman* (1990) it must be *fair, just and reasonable* to impose such a duty.

It is possible to denote three types of circumstance in which courts have recognised a duty of care to protect against pure economic loss. Thus a duty may arise in respect of negligent misstatement following *Hedley Byrne v. Heller and Partners* (1964). Negligent solicitors may owe a duty of care to disappointed beneficiaries where wills have been carelessly administered to the pursuers' loss following *White v. Jones* (1995). Finally a duty of care may arise following the case of *Junior Books Ltd v. Veitchi Co Ltd* (1983).

HEDLEY BYRNE LIABILITY

Heller and partners were a firm of advertising agents who had done a small amount of work for a client called Easipower. Easipower had plans for a far more extensive advertising campaign. Because there was some doubt regarding the financial position of Easipower, Heller sought a reference from Easipower's bankers, Hedley Byrne via their own bankers, National Provincial. On the strength of the positive reference provided by Hedley Byrne, Heller went ahead and placed adverts for Easipower. Subsequently Easipower went into liquidation leaving Heller with losses of £17,661.18/10d.

The judge at first instance and the Court of Appeal held that no duty of care was owed Heller by Hedley Byrne. In the House of Lords it was held that a duty of care did arise in the circumstances. However Heller were unable to recover damages, because the reference had been given with a specific disclaimer of responsibility on the part of Hedley Byrne.

Hedley Byrne sets out key requirements that must be satisfied before a duty of care can be said to arise in respect of negligent misstatement. These key points are necessary to satisfy the requirement of proximity. There must be an assumption of responsibility on the part of the person making the statement. The pursuer must have relied upon the defender to exercise such a degree of care as the circumstances required. It must have been reasonable for the pursuer to have relied on the exercise of care by the defender. The defender must have known or ought to have known that the pursuer would rely on the defender's statement. Moreover, since the case of *Caparo Industries v. Dickman* it is clear that it must have been reasonably foreseeable that the pursuer would act on the defender's advice or statement in a particular transaction or transaction of a particular type. It must be reasonably foreseeable to the defender that if insufficient care is taken in making the statement, loss on the part of the pursuer will result.

Hedley Byrne is a landmark decision in the law of negligence. This case over-ruled the earlier decision of the Court of Appeal in *Candler v. Crane Christmas & Co* (1951) in which it was held that a contractual or fiduciary relationship between the parties was necessary before a duty of care in negligence could arise. *Hedley Byrne* gave effect to Lord Justice Denning's dissenting opinion in *Candler*.

The rule in *Hedley Byrne* has been applied in a number of subsequent cases in which recovery of damages has been allowed in respect of negligent misstatement. For example in *Esso Petroleum Co v. Mardon* (1976) the owners of a petrol station made a careless representation to a prospective tenant regarding the potential throughput of petrol. The tenancy was taken in reliance on this statement. In court it was determined that the owners had held themselves out as having special expertise in circumstances which gave rise to a duty of care.

In *Martin v. Bell Ingram* (1986) it was held that a surveyor, conducting a house survey under a contract with a building society, owes a duty of care to the prospective buyer of the house provided that the surveyor knows the survey report will be used and relied upon by that particular buyer.

By contrast in *Caparo Industries plc v. Dickman* it was held that a negligently prepared company audit could not be used to found a claim when company shareholders successfully mounted a takeover bid on the strength of audited accounts. The accounts showed a profit of £1.3 million whereas the true figure was a loss of £0.46 million. No duty of care was owed the shareholders as potential investors. In *Hedley Byrne, Esso Petroleum* and *Martin* the party making the statement was aware not only of the identity of the party relying on the statement, but also knew of the particular transaction in respect of which reliance was placed on the statement. In order to satisfy the requirements of proximity, the negligent auditors in *Caparo* would have had to have known that these particular investors would rely on the audit for purposes of their takeover.

Hedley Byrne principles have been brought to bear in respect of negligent misstatement in personal references. See for example *Spring v. Guardian Assurance plc* (1995) and *Donlon Colonial Mutual Group (UK Holdings) Ltd* (1998).

LIABILITY OF SOLICITORS TO DISAPPOINTED BENEFICIARIES

In general a solicitor acting for a client acts under a contract and may be concurrently liable to the client in both contract and delict (see *Henderson v. Merrett Syndicates* (1997) on concurrent liability). However the solicitor owes no duty of care to third parties. Recent developments, not only in English law, but also in Commonwealth jurisdictions, the United States and some civilian countries such as France and Germany show that courts are increasingly willing to modify this position.

In *Ross v. Caunters* (1980) the Court of Appeal held that a solicitor owed a duty of care to an identified third party who had been named as beneficiary in a will. Because the will had been negligently executed by the solicitor the beneficiary failed to benefit from the intended legacy. Damages were awarded. The decision in this case owes more to *Donoghue* principles than it does to *Hedley Byrne* since the element of reliance, essential to *Hedley Byrne* liability was not present.

Scots law declined to follow the lead given by *Ross* in 1990 when, in *Weir v. JM Hodge & Son* (1990) it was held in the Outer House that a duty of care was not owed a disappointed beneficiary in circumstances similar to *Ross*. While it is clear from his opinion that he had some sympathy with the pursuer, Lord Weir considered himself bound by the earlier House of Lords decision in *Robertson v. Fleming* (1861). While Scots and English law were for a time out of step it is most likely that the position has changed since the House of Lords case of *White v. Jones* (1995).

In *White* the House of Lords ruled by a majority that disappointed beneficiaries could recover in tort in respect of a will that was not drawn up at all. Following a family dispute the deceased had instructed a will that disinherited his daughters. There was a reconciliation and the solicitor was instructed to draft a new will. The solicitor neglected to do this so that when the testator died the distribution of the estate was governed by the original will. The House of Lords declined to follow *Robertson* which was viewed as out of sympathy with current developments in a number of jurisdictions and *Ross v. Caunters* was approved.

There are a number of conceptual difficulties posed by the cases of *Ross* and *White* and these are fully discussed in *White* in the speech of Lord Goff. Nevertheless the current position may be viewed as broadly satisfactory on the grounds that liability extends only to beneficiaries whose existence will of course be known to the solicitor. Thus there is proximity between parties and the scope of liability is not indeterminate.

JUNIOR BOOKS LIABILITY

Finally the case of *Junior Books Ltd v. The Veitchi Co Ltd* (1983) must be noted. In *Junior Books* a subcontractor was held liable to the owner of premises in respect of the costs of replacing a defective floor. Despite the fact that the subcontractors had no direct contractual relationship with the owners and the loss was pure economic loss since the defective floor was neither dangerous nor likely to cause harm to persons or other property, the House of Lords allowed recovery of damages.

It was significant to the decision that Veitchi, the subcontractor was nominated by the agent of the Junior Books. Thus Veitchi would have known the identity of the owners and that Junior Books would rely on their skill and expertise. Accordingly they would have known that careless performance on their part would result in economic loss to Junior Books.

It may be noted that *Junior Books* dates from the period when *Anns v. Merton Borough Council* was in force. While *Junior Books* has not been over-ruled subsequent case law suggests strongly that it is most unlikely that recovery of pure economic loss in such circumstances will be allowed in future. There were factors in *Junior Books* that pointed to a greater degree of proximity between the parties than was the case in *D&F Estates v. Church*

Commissioners for England in which *Junior Books* was distinguished. However, it may be thought that *D&F Estates* rather than *Junior Books* indicates the approach that is likely to be taken by the courts in such circumstances for the foreseeable future.

---

4. NERVOUS SHOCK

INTRODUCTION

The term "nervous shock" is used as an alternative to psychiatric harm. Medically, the expression may be dubious. However, lawyers tend to persist in the term nervous shock as it indicates the way in which courts have approached this phenomenon. This is true historically and the idea of an immediate and overwhelming blow to the senses causing mental harm still informs current legal thinking.

Indeed, courts will only recognise claims for psychiatric harm caused through negligence where that harm is the result of some shocking, sudden and horrific event. Thus, recovery has been denied parents who suffered psychiatric illness when their child took three days to die (*Taylorson v. Shieldness Produce Ltd*, 1994 P.I.Q.R. 329). Similarly, a father who maintained a two-week vigil at the bedside of his dying son was unable to recover damages, because his subsequent illness was not attributable to a single shocking event (*Sion v. Hampstead Health Authority* [1994] 5 Med.L.R.). These cases may be contrasted with *Tredget v. Bexley Health Authority* [1994] 5 Med.L.R. 178 in which the birth and death two days later of a child born with serious injuries was treated effectively as a single event.

While courts have been circumspect about the possibility of spurious claims, modern psychiatry is such that there are physical symptoms that may be more easily faked than mental health problems. The law does indeed demand, for a relevant claim, that pursuers suffer some recognised psychiatric condition such as Post Traumatic Stress Disorder. Mere anxiety or emotional distress is not sufficient to found a claim (*Simpson v. ICI* (1983)).

Finally, it should be noted that there is a growing body of case law involving recovery of damages from employers in respect of stress related illness in the workplace. Such cases follow from *Walker v. Northumberland County Council* (1995). This is a related, but different area of liability from that under consideration in this chapter.

DEVELOPMENT OF LIABILITY IN NEGLIGENCE FOR NERVOUS SHOCK

Recognition of the principle of recovery

Initially, courts demonstrated much reluctance in recognising non-physical personal injury as reparable. The policy reason for this attitude is made clear through a number of judicial dicta to the effect that admitting such a form of loss would result in a barrage of spurious claims. At one time, loss in the form of psychiatric harm was simply viewed as too remote. Thus in *Victoria Railway Commissioners v. Coultas* (1888) the Privy Council refused damages to a lady who had suffered "severe nervous shock" and subsequent illness and miscarriage after a very narrow escape from being run down by a train. However, *Coultas* was not followed two years later in *Bell v. Great Northern Railway of Ireland* (1890). The Exchequer Division in Ireland awarded damages to a female train passenger who had suffered nervous shock through fear for her own safety. The railway company was held to be in breach of a duty to convey passengers not only safely, but securely.

In 1899 an award of £500 in damages was given in the Court of Session to a man who suffered nervous shock during a freak rail accident (*Wood v. NB Railway Co*). A train coming in the other direction carried a load of pit props that protruded beyond the width of the trucks. When the pursuer's train met the goods train the props broke through the carriage in which the pursuer was a passenger and brought his train to a violent halt. This case went to the House of Lords, but the issue there was whether the pursuer was barred from seeking damages in court having accepted an offer in settlement. The House of Lords did not determine an issue of whether nervous shock was reparable until *Bourhill v. Young* in 1943. In *Wood* the award made by the Lord Ordinary was not disturbed. Only the English judges appear to have doubted whether such loss was reparable.

That psychiatric harm is recoverable in principle was only clearly established in English law in *Dulieu v. White & Sons* (1901). The Divisional Court of the Kings Bench Division allowed recovery of damages to a woman who had suffered a severe shock when a horse van was negligently driven into the bar in which she worked. The plaintiff was pregnant at the time and later gave premature birth to a child who, as the law report puts it, was "born an idiot". *Dulieu* was subsequently followed in 1908 in the Scottish case of *Wallace v. Kennedy*.

Thus, at the beginning of the twentieth century it was clear that psychiatric harm in the form of nervous shock was not too remote to give rise to recovery in damages. Recovery at the time was restricted to those whose shock was caused by fear for their own personal safety rather than fear for the safety of others. Moreover, damages were recoverable even though nervous shock was unaccompanied by physical injury.

Reasonable foreseeability

The first case in which damages were recovered where the victim of shock was concerned, not for her own safety, but for that of her children was *Hambrook v. Stokes* in 1925. This was a majority decision of the Court of

Appeal. However, the status of *Hambrook* as an authority remained in doubt following *Bourhill v. Young*. *Bourhill* emphasised the importance of reasonable foreseeability of psychiatric harm to the pursuer before a duty of care could arise. As Lord Denning said 10 years later in *King v. Phillips* (1953): "...there can be no doubt since *Bourhill v. Young* that the test of liability for shock is foreseeability of injury by shock". In *King v. Phillips* the Court of Appeal denied damages to a mother who had witnessed a taxi driver negligently reversing over her son's tricycle. The plaintiff heard the boy scream from seventy to eighty yards away, but could not see the boy when the taxi stopped. In fact he was unharmed. Ostensibly, like Mrs Bourhill, the plaintiff was too far from the incident for a duty of care to be owed her. The unacknowledged reason for the decision was one of policy. The Court sought to restrict liability for fear of "opening the floodgates" to a large number of claims.

In 1967 liability for nervous shock was extended to rescuers. In *Chadwick v. British Transport Commission* the plaintiff suffered depression and eventually committed suicide following horrific experiences in aiding victims of the Lewisham train disaster. The view was taken that it was reasonably foreseeable that, in such an event, citizens would come to the rescue and so a duty of care was owed those who did. Moreover, the actions of a rescuer do not constitute a *novus actus interveniens* breaking the chain of causation between the negligent act and resultant harm. This is because the rescuer acts out of moral obligation so his or her involvement is not treated as voluntary. From a policy point of view it was thought undesirable to deny recovery to selfless and altruistic rescuers.

Extension of principle of recovery
In 1983 the House of Lords allowed recovery in damages to a mother who witnessed the immediate aftermath of a road accident in which her husband and two children were injured and one child was killed (*McLaughlin v. O'Brian*). The limiting principle in *Dulieu*, that the shock must result for fear for personal safety was rejected. The existence of the duty of care owed the plaintiff was based on reasonable foreseeability of psychiatric harm, but the Court was also concerned with policy. In order to limit potential claims it was held necessary to have witnessed the incident or its immediate aftermath directly. Mrs McLauchlin arrived at the hospital where her family were held two hours after the accident. In holding that she witnessed the immediate aftermath it was significant that the victims had not been cleaned up, nor had wounds been dressed.

THE CURRENT POSITION

It has been possible to categorise pursuers in terms of participants, bystanders and rescuers, or in terms of those shocked through fear for their own safety as opposed to those shocked through witnessing horrific events befall others. However, the critical distinction in the modern context is between primary and secondary victims. This follows from the House of Lords cases of *Page v. Smith* (1996) and *White v. Chief Constable of South Yorkshire* (1998). This distinction is not always easy to draw. Broadly, a primary victim is a person within the range of potential physical harm. A secondary victim is a person outwith the range of potential physical harm.

Thus, new cases have to be approached, not by identifying the pursuer as a participant, bystander or rescuer, but by enquiring whether the pursuer was within the range of potential physical harm. For example, a rescuer might be either a primary or secondary victim depending upon the circumstances. In *White* the respondent police officers had been involved in assisting victims of the Hillsborough disaster. They were not held entitled to damages as they had not been in physical danger themselves. They were not, therefore, primary victims and moreover were unable to satisfy the requirements for recovery demanded of secondary victims. By contrast in *Hale v. London Underground* (1992 11 B.M.L.R. 81) a fireman successfully recovered damages for nervous shock. He had assisted in the Kings Cross disaster while the incident was still occurring. He had been exposed to considerable danger. Subsequently he suffered horrendous nightmares and severe depression. On his return to work he was only able to do a desk job.

PRIMARY VICTIMS

In *Page v. Smith* a man suffered a re-occurrence of ME (myalgic encephalomyelitis) when the stationary car in which he was sitting was bumped by the defendant's car. Clearly drivers owe a duty of care to other drivers and pedestrians within the range of potential harm not to cause personal injury or damage their property. However it was arguable that while physical harm might have been reasonably foreseeable, psychiatric harm was not. Nevertheless, damages were awarded.

It follows from *Page* that where a duty of care not to cause physical injury is established, and psychiatric harm results from the defender's negligence, the defender will be liable. In the case of primary victims psychiatric harm need not be reasonably foreseeable. Of course physical harm must be reasonably foreseeable or there would be no duty, but physical harm need not materialise for a claim to be valid. Effectively, where primary victims are concerned, the concept of personal injury has been broadened to include psychiatric harm.

In order to claim as a primary victim the pursuer must be exposed to danger or must reasonably apprehend him or herself to be in danger.

SECONDARY VICTIMS

Secondary victims have not been exposed to physical danger themselves. Nevertheless, they have suffered nervous shock, typically as a consequence of witnessing horrific events that have befallen primary victims such as relatives or colleagues. The circumstances in which secondary victims may recover damages in respect of nervous shock are strictly limited and courts take a highly restrictive approach in such cases. In contrast to primary victims, no duty of care to guard against psychiatric harm will arise unless such harm is a reasonably foreseeable consequence of breach.

Reasonable foreseeability of psychiatric harm is a necessary, but not sufficient condition for the existence of a duty of care. In addition, secondary victims have to satisfy three further "proximity" requirements that were established by the House of Lords in the Hillsborough disaster case brought by relatives of the primary victims, *Alcock v. Chief Constable of South Yorkshire* (1992). No duty will arise unless: a tie of love and affection is established between the secondary and primary victim; the secondary victim is present at the event or its immediate aftermath; and perception of the event or its immediate aftermath must be direct. Direct perception means that the secondary victim must personally see or hear the event. If the pursuer is told of the incident by a third party the claim will not be met.

The tie of love and affection between primary and secondary victims may be readily presumed in some relationships, for example between husband and wife or parent and child. However, other relationships are not precluded so in theory recovery should be possible where the primary victim is the homosexual partner of the secondary victim or the parties are very close, but not united by any conventional category of relationship. The critical factor is not the type of relationship, but its strength and this is a matter upon which evidence may have to be led. In *Alcock* the first appellant, Robert Alcock lost his brother in law. Another appellant, Brian Harrison lost two brothers. Neither was able to recover in respect of nervous shock in the absence of evidence to show that their relationships with the deceased were particularly close.

Of those appellants whose ties with the primary victims could be presumed, their cases failed because they could not satisfy either or both of the other two proximity requirements. Some of the appellants did not arrive at the scene until some eight hours after the event and this was held to be too remote in time to count as presence at the aftermath. The direct perception requirement was not satisfied in some cases where the appellants had learned of the tragedy on TV or heard about it on the radio.

THE STATE OF THE LAW

The view was expressed in *Alcock* that it would not be in every case that all three proximity requirements would require to be satisfied. However, subsequent cases such as *Robertson v. Forth Road Bridge Joint Board* (1995) in which the pursuer watched his workmate and drinking buddy of 20 years fall to his death, and *McFarlane v. E.E. Caledonia Ltd* (1994) in which an oil worker on a supply vessel witnessed at close proximity the series of explosions on the Piper Alpha oil platform, demonstrate the highly restrictive approach taken by the courts where secondary victims are concerned. In neither case did the pursuer succeed. The pursuers were not held to have been involved in the events in a way that would have allowed recovery as primary victims. Their ties with the primary victims were not such as to allow recovery as secondary victims.

By contrast in *Young v. Charles Church (Southern) Ltd* (1997) the plaintiff was a scaffolder. When his back was turned a workmate shorted out an overhead power cable with a scaffolding pole. The plaintiff was held by the Court of Appeal to have been within the area of physical danger and recovered damages as a primary victim. However, the point has been made that his nervous shock appears to have been attributable more to witnessing the horrific accident that befell his mate rather than out of fear for personal safety. Considered in the light of *Robertson, McFarlane* and the subsequent case of *Hunter v. British Coal* (1998) Mr Young appears to have been treated by the courts with uncharacteristic generosity.

In the recent Scottish case of *Campbell v. North Lanarkshire County Council* (2000) the pursuer witnessed the horrific aftermath of a series of electrical explosions. The nature of their injuries rendered the appearance of the victims, with whom the pursuer had been working, particularly ghastly. The pursuer returned to the site of the explosion to assist the victims. The pleadings in court focussed upon whether or not the pursuer was a primary victim. Although he had left the scene shortly before the accident, when he returned the event was still continuing. On the basis of his pleadings he appears to have had reasonable grounds to believe himself in danger. Lord Reed allowed a proof before answer, taking the view that the case could not be determined upon pleadings alone. Before reaching a decision it was held necessary to hear evidence on both sides regarding the risks to which the pursuer was exposed.

The current state of the law has been subjected to much criticism. It has been argued (*inter alia* in Law Commission Report on Liability for Psychiatric Illness (1998) (Law Com. No. 249)) that of the three proximity requirements in *Alcock*, only the requirement of close ties of love and affection should be retained. Of the three requirements this one ties in most closely with the concept of reasonable foreseeability and arguably is sufficient to restrict potential claims. The law as it stands is criticised for producing arbitrary and in some instances unfair results. For example, a train delay could be sufficient to make the difference between recovery and non-recovery if a relative arrives at hospital or the scene of an accident too late to be counted as present at the immediate aftermath.

As a final point, in the case of *Attia v. British Gas* (1987) the defendant company had negligently installed a central heating system in the plaintiff's house. The plaintiff suffered nervous shock when she arrived home to find her house burning to the ground. She recovered damages on the basis of reasonable foreseeability alone.

---

5. VICARIOUS LIABILITY

INTRODUCTION

Vicarious liability concerns the liability of one party for the delictual acts or omissions of another. It can be explained as a modification to the general rule, *culpa tenet suos auctores* (fault binds its authors). Two other maxims are commonly used to justify this modification, *qui facit per alium facit per se* (where one does a thing through the instrumentality of another, he is held as having done it himself) and *respondeat superior* (let the master answer).

In short, while it is normally the case that parties will only be liable for their own conduct, vicarious liability may arise where a delict is committed by a person acting on another's behalf. Where a servant (employee) commits a delict the master (employer) can be called upon to answer for it.

Vicarious liability operates in employment, in agency and in partnership. In all these situations there are relationships in which one party acts on behalf of another. So the employer may be vicariously liable for the acts of employees, the principal for the acts of agents and the other partners for the acts of a single partner. Most of the case law concerns the employer/employee relationship, but similar considerations apply to the other relationships. In agency for example the criterion for vicarious liability is whether the agent has acted within the scope of his or her authority.

Vicarious liability is not so much a matter of legal principle as policy. Where an employer conducts an enterprise that creates risks for others, it is fair that the employer should pay for the consequences of the risks when they materialise. The employer does, after all, take the benefits of the enterprise. The fact that the enterprise is conducted through the instrumentality of others (employees do the work) does not absolve the employer from meeting whatever liabilities arise from the conduct of the enterprise. Moreover, vicarious liability operates as a prompt to employers to promote safe conduct and practices in carrying out the enterprise.

The practical effect of vicarious liability is to give the victim a defender worth suing. Imagine you suffer extensive injuries caused by the negligent driving of a fork lift truck in your local do-it-yourself store. The delinquent truck driver is on a relatively low wage and has no financial assets to speak of. He or she could not hope to compensate you for your losses. On the other hand the employer, a corporation with substantial assets and a turnover of many millions, is in a position easily to meet your claims. Moreover, the employer will probably have insurance that covers such losses. Where the victim also is an employee, insurance is compulsory under the Employer's Liability (Compulsory Insurance) Act 1969.

It is important to note that vicarious liability arises not only from negligence, but also from intentional wrongdoing. For example, in *Morris v. CW Martin & Sons Ltd* (1966) an employee committed the tort of conversion by stealing a mink stole deposited with the defendants for cleaning. The employers were vicariously liable to the plaintiff for her loss. In *Photo Production Ltd v. Securicor Transport Ltd* (1980) an employee deliberately started a fire that burned down the factory he was supposed to be guarding. It was held that vicarious liability arose. (See also *Taylor v. Glasgow District Council* (1997) which involved fraud by a building control officer).

Where one party is held vicariously liable the delinquent is not released from liability. Vicarious liability is imposed in addition to the liability of the party at fault. Liability is joint and several. The pursuer may elect to sue either or both parties. In theory the vicariously liable party may recover damages paid to the pursuer from the party at fault (*Lister v. Romford Ice* (1957)). In practice this seldom happens.

It should be noted that even where vicarious liability is not established, a case against the defender may be maintained if it can be established that the defender was personally liable to the pursuer. It is not unusual to see a plea of vicarious liability advanced as an alternative to an averment of personal liability. An example would be where a person is injured on trade premises by a falling slate dropped by an employee who is fixing the roof. The employer might be vicariously liable for the negligence of the employee, but could also be personally liable as occupier for harm done due to the state of the building (Occupiers' Liability (Scotland) Act 1960).

It is not in every case that employers will be held vicariously liable. If you step on a landmine, laid as an illegal remedy against dog fouling in my front garden, there will be no point in seeking reparation from my employer, the University of Dundee. The delict in this example bears no relation to my employment. Of course there are many situations where the issue of vicarious liability is not so clear cut as in this example. For vicarious liability to arise, the delict must be sufficiently connected to the delinquent's employment. The basic features involved in determining whether conduct gives rise to vicarious liability will be considered below.

The other difficulty found in vicarious liability is in determining for whom the employer is liable. In general employers are vicariously liable for employees, *i.e.* those under a contract of service and not for independent contractors, those under a contract for services. However, allocating particular relationships to either category is not always as straightforward as might be thought. This distinction is also considered below.

EMPLOYEE ACTING WITHIN THE SCOPE OF EMPLOYMENT

A good starting point for a Scots text is a dictum of Lord President Clyde in *Kirby v. NCB* (1958). An English text would start with *Salmond on Torts*, the source from which Lord Clyde derived his formulation:

"In the decisions four different types of situation have been envisaged as guides to the solution of this problem. [1] In the first place, if the master actually authorised the particular act, he is clearly liable for it. [2] Secondly, where the workman does some work which he is appointed to do, but does it in a way which his master has not authorised and would not have authorised had he known of it, the master is nevertheless still responsible for the servant's act is still within the scope of his employment. [3] On the other hand in the third place, if the servant is employed only to do a particular work or a particular class of work, and he does something outside the scope of that work, the master is not responsible for any mischief the servant may do to a third party. [4] Lastly, if the servant uses his master's time or his master's tools for his own purposes, the master is not responsible."

Categories [1] and [4] are relatively clear. The difficulties that arise in practice concern the distinction between [2] and [3]. An unauthorised mode of doing an authorised act [2] gives rise to vicarious liability, but an act that is outwith the scope of employment, *i.e.* completely independent of the employer's business [3] does not. However, independent acts may give rise to vicarious liability if they are sufficiently connected with the employer's business. This is considered further below under "recent developments".

In *Kirby* the pursuer was a mine employee who had gone to a part of the pit away from his working place for a smoke. The defender, the employer, was not liable for the injuries sustained in an explosion when a match was lit by an unidentified miner. Going for a smoke was not in any way connected with the pursuer's work, it was done purely for his own purposes and pleasure and, incidentally, was in breach of statute. The pursuer had acted outwith the scope of his employment.

Still on the subject of smoking, the difference between [2] and [3] may be illustrated by contrasting *Kirby* with *Century Insurance Co Ltd v. Northern Ireland Road Transport Board* (1942). In an act of monumental stupidity the driver of a fuel tanker lit a cigarette and discarded a match while draining 300 gallons of petrol from his tanker into a garage storage tank. The resulting explosion damaged the garage owner's car and several houses. In this case the driver was acting within the scope of his employment and his employers were therefore vicariously liable. Lighting the cigarette was an unauthorised act, but done while the driver was doing his job. As Lord Chancellor Viscount Simon observed, "They also serve who stand and wait". It was the driver's duty to watch over the delivery. He was negligent in the discharge of his duty, but he was actively discharging his duty while negligent, therefore he was acting within the scope of his employment. *Century Insurance* falls within [2].

The reason *Kirby* was unsuccessful in his claim was that he was "off on a frolic of his own", rather than acting within the scope of his employment. Similarly, in *McLean v. Remploy Ltd* (1994) the pursuer was the victim of a practical joke, played on him by other, unidentified employees who had tied a length of yarn across a corridor. The Lord Ordinary (Cameron) held that employers could not be held vicariously liable for such frolics. However, such cases turn on their own circumstances and in *Harrison v. Michelin Tyre Co Ltd* (1985) the defender was found vicariously liable when an employee was injured by a prank. The critical feature has been whether or not the act can be deemed to be within the scope of employment.

The Race Relations Act 1976, s.32(1) states that "Anything done by a person in the course of his employment shall be treated for the purposes of this Act (except as regards offences thereunder) as done by his employer as well as him, whether or not it was done with the employer's knowledge or approval..."

When Raymondo Jones sought damages in respect of racial abuse carried out by two fellow employees the Industrial Tribunal held the employer vicariously liable by virtue of s.32. This decision was reversed by the Employment Appeal Tribunal on the basis that the abusers could not be described as acting in the course of their employment. Racial abuse was not an unauthorised mode of working, it was a series of independent acts. The House of Lords, in seeking to give effect to the intention of Parliament, to eliminate racial discrimination, held the employer liable. The words "in the course of his employment", were to be given their ordinary everyday meaning and not construed in accordance with common law rules on vicarious liability. Accordingly, where an employee is subjected to racial abuse by fellow employees, the employer will be vicariously liable under statute and the common law does not apply (*Jones v. Tower Boot Co Ltd* (1997)).

The courts have demonstrated a clear tendency to find vicarious liability so long as the employer's purposes are being pursued when the delict is committed. This is so even though the employer's rules have been broken. In *Rose v. Plenty* (1975) a milkman hired a 13-year-old boy to assist with deliveries in flagrant breach of dairy policy. The boy was injured when the milkman drove the float negligently. The dairy was found vicariously liable since the boy's presence on the float was in pursuance of the employer's business.

The following three examples concern drivers who deviated from their most direct routes in the course of carrying out their employers' instructions. In all these cases employers were found vicariously liable on the basis that the delinquent employees were conducting authorised work in an unauthorised way. Each case demonstrates in successive fashion the extent to which courts will go in order to hold that acts are within the scope of employment and therefore employers are liable. In *Angus v. Glasgow Corporation* (1977) a lorry driver took a short deviation from his route in order to collect his spectacles from home. He collided with a car. The car driver sued the lorry driver's employers successfully in negligence. In *McLeod v. South of Scotland Electricity Board* (1982) a van struck and damaged a footbridge that the pursuers were constructing. The driver had been authorised to take the vehicle home, but when a few hundred yards from home he had gone out of his way to drop off a fellow employee and had then taken a further diversion to visit his mother in law. The Lord Ordinary (Wylie) held that the original authorised purpose of the journey had not been wholly superseded.

The final case, *Williams v. Hemphill* (1966) which went all the way to the House of Lords, shows the most outrageous deviation. A driver was employed to take a boys' brigade company from Benderloch in Knapdale home to Glasgow. Some of the boys prevailed upon the driver to go to Dollar in Clackmannanshire. This was in order to see once again a party of girl guides whom the boys had helped with luggage at Connel station. Instead of turning down the A82 at Crianlarich which would have taken them down Loch Lomondside and into Glasgow by Dumbarton the driver headed by the A85 and A84 for Stirling from where he took an eccentric route for Dollar by the south bank of the Forth and Kincardine. This deviation took the party directly away from Glasgow. Through negligent driving the lorry was overturned on a corner heading into Dollar and there were injuries and fatalities. At all stages of the litigation it was held that the employer was vicariously liable. The dominant purpose of the journey was transportation of the boys to Glasgow, the driver was still engaged in this purpose and the deviation by Dollar was not an independent journey.

RECENT DEVELOPMENTS

The three driver cases and *Rose v. Plenty* demonstrate that a broad view is taken of whether conduct is within the scope of employment. Nevertheless, problems have emerged with the old approach that seeks to distinguish between unauthorised modes of doing work and independent acts. A new approach to determining vicarious liability has been pioneered in the Canadian Supreme Court and accepted and applied by the House of Lords in the English case of *Lister v. Hesley Hall Ltd* (2001). The new approach is very much a development on the old rather than a departure and there is no reason to suppose that it will not be followed in Scotland.

The issue underlying vicarious liability cases is whether, as a matter of policy and in the circumstances, it is fair and just to impose on the employer liability for the conduct complained of. Courts should now be explicit about this rather than veiling such determinations beneath technical distinctions. Whether circumstances give rise to vicarious liability depends on the outcome of the close connection test. Under this test it must be determined whether an act is *sufficiently connected* to employment for it to be fair and just to hold the employer vicariously liable.

The application of this test can be explored through the case law in which the new approach was developed. In *Bazley v. Curry* (1999) an employee in a residential care home sexually abused one of the children in his care. The acts were sufficiently connected with his employment for the employers to be held vicariously liable. By contrast in *Jacobi v. Griffiths* (1999) an employee at a children's' recreational club sexually abused a brother and sister who attended the club. With the exception of one incident, the abuse took place at the defendant's home. The fact that the defendant had met the children at the club did not establish a sufficiently close connection between the acts and employment. The employers were held by a majority of the Canadian Supreme Court not to be vicariously liable. In *Lister v. Hesley Hall Ltd* (2001) the warden of a school boarding house sexually abused children in his care in a systematic fashion. There was sufficient connection between the acts and employment for the employers to be held vicariously liable.

The logic of these decisions is clear, but the results are not necessarily those that would be reached under the old approach. This may be demonstrated by reference to *Trotman v. North Yorkshire County Council* (1999). The deputy headmaster of a special school was charged with responsibility for caring for a disabled teenager on a foreign holiday. The teacher sexually abused the boy. In seeking to distinguish between unauthorised modes of work and independent acts the Court of Appeal found the employers were not vicariously liable. This was not a wrong decision in a legal sense though it produced an unjust result. Far from being an unauthorised mode of carrying out a duty the acts were held to be a negation of the duty and thus independent. The new approach, which takes into account the nature and purpose of the act along with the context and circumstances in which it occurred, should avoid such decisions in the future. The broad approach to vicarious liability demonstrated in *Rose v. Plenty* and *Williams v. Hemphill* is maintained, but now the courts will concentrate on sufficient connection between acts and employment and the old distinction between unauthorised modes and independent acts becomes redundant. *Trotman* was overruled by the House of Lords in *Lister*.

It can be predicted that where a person charged with the care of children in residence uses their position to commit acts of sexual abuse within the home the employer will be liable. On the other hand if a schoolteacher abuses school pupils in his own home the fact that he has met the children at his work may not establish a sufficient connection between the acts and employment to render the employers vicariously liable. However, a case of this nature is a marginal example. If a relationship of trust and intimacy was developed in the classroom courts might well hold a sufficient connection. The result will depend on all the circumstances of the case. Where an employee uses their position working alongside another to conduct a campaign of sexual harassment, for example where two persons work in close proximity and one continually contrives to brush up against the other, there is little doubt that the employer will be vicariously liable. However, a party may conduct a campaign of harassment against a fellow employee without sufficient connection between employment and the acts for vicarious liability to arise. See for example, *Ward v. Scotrail Railways Ltd* (1999), approved by the House of Lords in *Lister*.

Since the peculiar circumstances of each case play a critical role in determining sufficient connection, it is difficult to make general predictions on the likely outcomes of potential cases.

FOR WHOM IS THE EMPLOYER LIABLE?

Vicarious liability is dependent upon the relationship between the delinquent and the liable party. Employers are liable for the delicts of employees, but not for those of independent contractors. In many instances the distinction between employees and contractors is easily made. In employment the parties are linked by a contract of employment which is either permanent or for a fixed term. The contract terminates at the expiry of the term or following the period of notice according to the contract terms. Equally, the employee may be dismissed. This is a contract of service (*locatio operarum*). A contractor on the other hand is on a contract to perform some specific task or service. The contract terminates when the obligations have been discharged, normally when the work has been completed or the service rendered and payment has been made. This is a contract for services (*locatio operis faciendi*).

The difference may be illustrated by comparing a taxi driver, whom one employs in order to get from A to B on a one-off basis, with a chauffeur, employed to drive one's Bentley wherever and whenever one wishes to go. The former is a contractor. The latter is an employee.

Problems arise where the nature of the contract between the delinquent and the employer is unclear or ambiguous. One test that has been used to determine the distinction between employees and contractors concerns the element of control. According to the control test, where the employer can tell the other party not only what to do, but also how to do it the relationship is one of employment. While this approach works well in respect of unskilled work it is less useful where work is skilled or specialised. For example, when the server is down in the Law Department it is the job of the network supervisor to get it running again, but neither the Head of Department, the Dean nor the Principal himself can tell the supervisor how to do it. Nevertheless the supervisor is an employee.

There is a wide range of factors that can be taken into account in determining the nature of the relationship. The element of control may be a factor depending on circumstances. Other factors include: the extent to which the person is integrated into the organisation as a whole; whether the party runs a commercial risk; the intention of the parties; whether payment is in the form of regular wages or salary or for "the job"; whether employers' national insurance contributions are made; whether tax is deducted as PAYE or the party makes their own tax arrangements; pension arrangements; and the way in which the contract may be terminated.

By taking into account multiple factors according to the circumstances rather than adhering to a rigid test the courts are able to produce just results in a multiplicity of differing contractual arrangements. So for example, in *Short v. J&W Henderson Ltd* (1946) a docker was held to be an employee of the defending company despite working arrangements very different from that which we would naturally think of as employment.

The defenders were responsible for shipping and unloading a cargo of cement at Campeltown harbour. Dockers at Campeltown were organised so that, whenever a ship was due in, a sufficient number of dockers to unload the cargo was allocated on a strict rota basis. The allocation was made by the local trade union secretary, himself a docker who took part on the rota in turn. There was no foreman or any docker in charge. The shippers paid a lump sum for the discharge of the cargo to a broker who in turn paid that sum to whichever docker had been sent to receive payment. The dockers involved on each occasion then divided the money equally between themselves. The broker stamped the National Health and Unemployment Insurance card of any docker employed for the first time that week, seeking the employers' contribution from the shippers. When three dockers were injured in an accident, it was held in the House of Lords that each docker was under an individual contract of employment with the shipper. A number of factors were deemed relevant and the requirement of control was held satisfied by the fact that the brokers, as agents of the employers, had regularly attended the unloading. This pointed to supervision. While there had never been any need to dismiss or suspend a docker it was found that had such a need occurred this power would have been exercised by the broker on the shipper's behalf.

In one further example, *United Wholesale Grocers Ltd v. Sher* (1993), warehouse owners contracted with the defender for joinery work. Sher entrusted the job to three workmen who were paid daily without any deductions for tax or national insurance. Allegedly, one of the workmen negligently discarded a cigarette that caused a fire in the warehouse. The pursuers sought to hold Sher vicariously liable. In the Outer House Lord Cullen had to determine whether the workmen were employees or independent contractors. While the control exercised by Sher over the way in which the work was done was an important factor, it was not conclusive. This was particularly so since supervision of the men was not necessary in the circumstances. The status of the workmen depended on assessment of all relevant factors. Sher supplied the materials, but the workmen supplied their own tools. It fell to be considered whether the work carried out should be regarded as part and parcel of a business carried out by Sher, or as part of

what the men were doing on their own account. Lord Cullen came to the
conclusion that they were employees of Sher carrying out work on the
warehouse that Sher had contracted to undertake.

In general, employers cannot be held vicariously liable for the delicts of
independent contractors although they may become personally liable to their
own employees if an incompetent contractor is appointed in breach of the
employer's duty to take reasonable care for the safety of employees.

There is one exceptional case in which an employee's widow was able to
recover from his employer for the delict of an independent contractor, despite
a finding that there was no element of personal liability. The pursuer's
husband was a quarry manager who died while checking an electrode spark
in a burner. The contractor was an electrician who fired both ignition and
fuel buttons on the burner when testing it. The electrician was the only one
employed at the quarry and he was perpetually available to the quarry.
Working at the quarry took up most of his time. Nevertheless, the Inner
House determined that the electrician was an independent contractor, but the
defenders were vicariously liable for his act (*Marshall v. William Sharp &
Sons Ltd* (1991)). This case is regarded as controversial although it has been
argued that the decision can be supported on grounds of the degree of control
exercised by the defenders over the electrician.

PRO HAC VICE EMPLOYMENT

Finally, the situation sometimes arises when courts have to determine which
of two different employers is vicariously liable for the delict of an employee.
This arises where an employee is lent out or hired. In general, liability rests
with the employer with whom the employee has a contract of employment.
The employer who borrows the person will only become vicariously liable if
it can be established that full control over not only what the employee does,
but how he or she does it, has passed to the borrowing employer.

This rule is not varied by any contractual agreement between the two
employers. Thus, even though a contract provides that the party is to be
regarded as a servant of the borrowing employer, this cannot be relied upon
in an issue with a third party who was not a party to the contract (*Mersey
Docks and Harbour Board v. Coggins & Griffith (Liverpool) Ltd* (1947)). In
this House of Lords case the defendants, a firm of stevedores, borrowed a
crane and driver from the Harbour Board. It was held that while the
stevedores told the crane driver what to do, the way in which he did it was a
matter within his own discretion. This discretion had been delegated to him
by the Harbour Board. When the crane driver negligently injured an
employee of Coggins & Griffith, the Harbour Board were held vicariously
liable. (See also *Moir v. Wide Arc Services Ltd* (1987)).

6. DEFAMATION

INTRODUCTION

People are entitled to conduct their daily lives without having their characters besmirched or their reputation dragged through the mud. Citizens have a legitimate and legally protected interest in what Stair described as: fame, reputation and honour (Stair, *Institute* 1, ix, 4). A person's interest in their reputation is a reparable interest. Accordingly, where that interest is harmed, damages may be sought. Equally interdict may be sought in order to prevent an injurious publication or broadcast from taking place.

The interest in honour and reputation is protected primarily by the law of defamation. There is a related action of verbal injury that is similar, but not identical. Indeed, in some circumstances the law of negligence may provide a remedy.

In modern society personal honour is perhaps less important to most of us than it would have been in the Victorian and Edwardian periods. Norrie (*Defamation and Related Actions in Scots Law*, 1995) has calculated that in terms of numbers, defamation actions reached a peak in the 20 years between 1890 and 1910. Since then cases have become relatively rare. The prime reasons given by Norrie for the relative infrequency of defamation cases are: the demise of the late Victorian idea of honour; the lack of legal aid for defamation actions; the fact that almost no use was made of civil juries in Scotland during the twentieth century; and the modest level of damages awarded in the Scottish courts. Doubtless the last two points are related. The very high levels of damages sometimes set in England by juries are not found this side of the border where civil juries are relatively seldom used.

In English law a distinction is drawn between slander and libel. Broadly, slander may be described as defamation in a transitory form such as speech. Libel may be described as defamation in a permanent form, such as writing. Libel is a criminal offence as well as an actionable tort. Slander gives rise only to civil liability on proof of actual damage. In practice this distinction presents English law with considerable difficulty. No such distinction is drawn in the Scots law of defamation. Defamation in modern Scots law is purely civil although historically there were criminal elements.

ESTABLISHING DEFAMATION

In a nutshell there are three fundamental elements of defamation. The statement must be defamatory, it must be false and there must be malice. It has been said that there must be loss, but personal affront is sufficient to amount to loss, there need be no patrimonial or economic loss. The only further requirement is that the statement must have been communicated. In

England, to be actionable, a statement must be communicated to a third party. In Scotland the requirement for communication can be satisfied by communication to the pursuer (*Ramsay v. Maclay* (1890)). The Scots approach to the rule on communication reflects the availability of *solatium* for affront or injury to feelings and the fact that there need be no patrimonial loss.

Defamatory capacity

Because malice and falsity are presumed, the focus of the pursuer's effort is likely to be on establishing the defamatory capacity of the statement complained of and the fact that he or she has been defamed. Whether a statement has the capacity to defame is a question of law. Whether the statement has actually defamed the pursuer is a question of fact.

Whether words have a defamatory capacity may be determined by the application of a test laid down by Lord Atkin in *Sim v. Stretch* (1936). "Would the words tend to lower the plaintiff in the estimation of right-thinking members of society generally?"

The test is thus objective. The issue is not what the pursuer understands the words to mean, neither is it relevant to consider what the defender meant by the words. Whether a statement is defamatory is determined by the views of "right-thinking" people. Of course, the court determines what "right-thinking" people think. "Right-thinking" people are reasonable persons who do not hold prejudices.

This brings us to the issue of innuendo. That is the way in which a meaning may be attributed to words that is not present on the face of the statement. For example the statement that X is a thief is prima facie defamatory. The statement that X holds a surprising quantity of electrical goods in a lock up garage is not. However, depending on the circumstances in which the statement is made it may bear the innuendo that either X is a thief or X deals in stolen goods. The onus lies on the pursuer to establish that the statement complained of bears the innuendo contended for.

The question that must be asked is, as Lord Anderson put it in *Duncan v. Scottish Newspapers Ltd* (1929): "[W]ould a reasonable man, reading the publication complained of, discover in it matter defamatory of the pursuer? Or, put otherwise, the question is, What meaning would the ordinary reader of the newspaper put upon the paragraph which the pursuer complained of?"

There is also a subjective element in the test for defamation. In determining defamatory capacity courts must take into account the type of person likely to have heard or read the statement, the personal circumstances of the pursuer and all the circumstances in which the statement is made. For example, the statement that the pursuer is a hard-drinking brute with an expansive repertoire of obscene verse who handles balls better than Gavin Hastings might well be defamatory if applied to a choirmaster and published in the Church of Scotland periodical, *Life & Work*. Whereas the same statement applied to a player and printed in a rugby programme might be both intended and regarded as complimentary. The point is that what may be deeply injurious in one context can be unobjectionable in another. The law takes context into account.

Malice and innocent defamation

While liability in defamation is based on malice, the pursuer is not required to prove malice on the part of the defender. Once the statement complained of is established as defamatory, malice is presumed from the harmful nature of the words used. This presumption is rebutted where the defence of qualified privilege applies and so in such cases malice does have to be shown.

The presumption of malice in defamation is one aspect of the law that might be thought to be unsatisfactory. It offends against the general idea of no liability without fault. This is particularly so since liability attaches not only to the person making the defamatory statement, but also to those who repeat or disseminate the statement. This obviously extends to newspaper editors and to broadcasters, but also includes bookshops, libraries and the operators of web pages. The ability of such persons to verify facts or check for defamatory content may be very limited. Despite the absence of any malicious intent to injure, the innocent disseminator of a defamatory statement may nevertheless be held liable. Where defamation is innocent the law extends a defence to persons who can show that they were not the author, editor or publisher of the offending statement. They must show that reasonable care was taken in relation to publication and further, that they did not know and had no reason to believe their actions caused or contributed to the publication of a defamatory statement (Defamation Act 1996, s.1).

The classic example of innocent defamation is the case of *Hulton v. Jones* (1910) in which the author of a novel created a fictional character with the unlikely name of Artemus Jones. Unfortunately for the author there was a real Artemus Jones. Doubly unfortunate was the fact that Artemus Jones was a barrister. The defendant was liable notwithstanding the fact that the defamation complained of was entirely innocent.

Falsity

Defamatory statements are presumed to be false. Therefore there is no onus on the pursuer to establish the falsity of what has been said. The defender may lead the defence of *veritas* in which case the onus rests on the defender to prove the truth of the statement. If the statement is true, then no action lies in defamation since a defamatory statement is by definition false. Accordingly, *veritas* is a complete defence.

TYPES OF DEFAMATORY STATEMENT

The types of statement or imputation that have given rise to actions in defamation can be listed thus: criminality; immorality; professional incompetence; financial unsoundness; disease or disability; and aspersions against public character (Norrie, 1995). However it must be noted that there is absolutely no requirement that a defamatory statement must fall under any one of these headings.

Criminality

False imputations of criminal conduct have proven a fertile source of litigation. Nevertheless it is not every imputation of criminal conduct that will give rise to liability in defamation since the test of lowering the pursuer in the estimation of "right-thinking" people must be satisfied. All crimes do not carry the same level of social stigma. Accusations or imputations of murder (*Monson v. Tussauds* (1894)), theft (*Neville v. C&A Modes* (1945)), lewd and libidinous practices or shameless indecency will clearly have the effect of reducing the social esteem in which a person is held. In *Gecas v. Scottish Television* (1992) an action was brought by a party accused of involvement in the liquidation of Jews during the Second World War. Such an accusation is defamatory, but this case was successfully defended on grounds of *veritas*. The pursuer is at the time of writing subject to extradition proceedings brought by Lithuania. There are other crimes which would fail Lord Atkin's test, so for example, if a person is wrongly accused of a parking violation this would not be defamatory since such an accusation would not have the effect of lowering the accused in the esteem of others. Other crimes fall into a grey area so if the accusation is of driving over the legal limit for alcohol this would be considered defamatory now, but might well not have been so forty, thirty or even twenty years ago. Would people think less of you if they believed you had a speeding conviction? Would the answer to this question differ according to whether you were accused of driving at 85 mph on the motorway or at 160 mph in a 30 limit on a Yamaha R1? How would you regard a person whom you believed had been convicted of failure to obtain a TV license?

Immorality

Lord Atkin's "right-thinking" people test is sufficiently flexible to allow for the fact that what tends to lower a person in the estimation of other people changes over time. Nowhere is this clearer than in the context of immorality. The objective element of the test allows for social attitudes changing over time. Thus, while it has been held defamatory to imply pre-marital sexual relations (*Morrison v. Ritchie & Co* (1902)) or a "lack of womanly delicacy" (*Cuthbert v. Linklater* (1935)) it is very doubtful if any such implication would now lower the pursuer in social esteem. Similarly, in *Brownlie v. Thomson* (1859) damages were obtained in respect of the pursuer having been called a "blackguard". Blackguard means scoundrel, an insult which carried weight at the time but which has passed out of common usage.

Not only do notions of morality change, but in a modern pluralistic society it becomes increasingly difficult to establish the likely reaction of "right-thinking" people since general agreement on some aspects of morality is conspicuously lacking. For example, in certain sections of society it would be deeply insulting and defamatory to suggest that a man is uncircumcised. Nevertheless this sort of consideration can be taken into account by the law through the subjective element of the test for defamation.

Accordingly, precedents for a particular imputation being held defamatory are an incomplete guide to whether similar statements are actionable today or in the future. Actions founded on imputations of immorality were relatively uncommon during the twentieth century in comparison with the nineteenth. Nevertheless imputations on a person's moral character may continue to found actions, the success of which will depend on how the aspersion is viewed by "right-thinking" people and of course, on the context. "Right-thinking" people would probably not shun an individual purely on grounds of homosexuality (*Quilty v. Windsor* (1999)) or a couple who are believed to be cohabiting without being married. They might well lower their esteem of someone believed to be conducting an adulterous relationship, or working as a prostitute. In *Finburgh v. Moss's Empires Ltd* (1908) the manager of a theatre asked a married couple to leave, calling the wife a "notorious prostitute". One can imagine the degree of personal affront this must have caused. The wife succeeded in recovering damages, the husband did not. The court in 1908 did not find the suggestion that a man kept company with a prostitute defamatory.

Professional competence and professional misconduct

These types of defamatory statement do continue to give rise to litigation. Imputations against a person's conduct in a professional context are likely to have economic as well as social implications. Moreover, professionals may be members of professional bodies willing to fund litigation. There are many examples of cases involving imputations of professional incompetence in the case law ranging from a doctor accused of "gross negligence" (*Simmers v. Morton* (1900)) to a market gardener accused of letting weeds over-run his plots (*Cadzow v. District Commissioners of Edinburgh* (1914)). Professional misconduct is slightly different since there need be no suggestion of incompetence. In such instances defamation consists of an allegation which is damaging because of the pursuer's professional position. For example, to accuse a person of being a racist might or might not be defamatory depending on the context. If an allegation is made that a police officer was motivated by racism to arrested a person then that is defamatory (*Fraser v. Mirza* (1993)).

Financial unsoundness

Allegations of financial unsoundness may offer no comment on the moral character or social acceptability of a person. However, any such aspersion may have severe detrimental economic consequences. The victim may no longer be able to obtain credit, credit already extended to him or her may be withdrawn. Allegations of this type are actionable as defamation although there is some difficulty in reconciling this with the test which requires lowering in social esteem. It has been suggested that defamation operates to protect a person's commercial character as well as their private persona.

Disease or disability

In the past the view has been taken that an imputation of insanity or "loathsome disease" or even male impotence is actionable as defamation. However this view does not accord with the view that what is defamatory is that which tends to lower the person in the esteem of right thinking people. Right thinking people are doubtless sympathetic to the ill. Indeed, the twentieth century yielded no cases raised on such a basis. An allegation of illness, whether mental or physical ought not to be regarded as defamatory. On the other hand an allegation that a person suffers from a sexually transmitted disease might bear the innuendo of an allegation of sexual profligacy which might indeed be defamatory.

Aspersions against public character

Politicians and persons in public office in general must bear a great deal of criticism and even abuse. Such elements are part and parcel of public life and a great deal of latitude is accorded those who seek to criticise. After all, the public has a legitimate interest in the criticism of public office bearers whom they either elect directly or who are appointed by elected persons or bodies. Depending on the circumstances in which criticism is made, comments may attract qualified privilege in which case the presumption of malice does not operate. However a distinction has to be drawn between attacks on public and private character. It may not be defamatory to criticise the way in which a council leader does his or her job, but it is defamatory to suggest that he or she is corrupt or enervated by base motives. In short the latitude given to criticism of the council leader *qua* public officer is not extended to criticism of the council leader *qua* citizen.

It may be noted that the Representation of the People Act 1983, s.106(1) makes it a criminal offence to make a false statement about the personal character or conduct of a candidate for Parliament before or during an election. Any such charge may be defended if it can be shown that there were reasonable grounds for belief in the statement and that the accused did in fact believe it to be true.

DEFENCES TO DEFAMATION

Veritas

Since by definition a defamatory statement is untrue, *veritas* (truth) affords a complete defence. The onus is on the defender to prove the truth of the allegation. When applied successfully this defence rebuts the presumption of falsity.

In rixa

Rixa means a quarrel or brawl. Words uttered in the heat of the moment may be defensible on grounds that they were not seriously intended. It follows that this defence is only available in respect of spoken and not written defamation. The classic example of this defence is *Christie v. Robertson* (1899). A misunderstanding arose at an auction when two men both thought they had bought the same horse. When one of them led it away a quarrel ensued in which one man said of the other that he "should have been in the hands of the police twenty times in the last five years". The defence succeeded.

Vulgar abuse and sarcasm

Statements that are abusive or sarcastic are treated similarly to words uttered *in rixa*, they are not viewed as seriously intended. Thus great scope is allowed satirical television programmes, magazines and cartoons to lampoon public figures without fear of attracting litigation. Reasonable viewers or readers will not regard mockery or abuse as serious allegation. Similarly football referees cannot raise defamation actions in respect of statements questioning the marital status of their parents or imputations of membership of the masonic lodge.

Fair retort

If an allegation is made against a person that person is entitled to reply. If the reply contains defamatory elements then it may found an action for defamation, but there is no presumption of malice. Therefore the pursuer will have to establish malice on the part of the defender. The fact that a reply has been made is suggestive of a desire to protect reputation and does not infer malice (see for example *Gray v. SSPCA* (1890)). In order to count as a fair retort the reply must be kept within the bounds of relevance. In *Blair v. Eastwood* (1935) the defender overstepped the boundaries of fair retort when he was accused by the pursuer of having fathered her child. He in turn accused the pursuer of having had sex with at least two other men. This was not a fair retort.

Fair Comment

The defence of fair comment arises in the context of comments or reviews on matters in which the public has an interest. As a matter of policy the law allows considerable freedom of expression for example when works of art are reviewed or commented upon. The subject of the comment or review might be a book, a play, a painting, a sculpture, music or even a building. These are examples. The defence is not restricted to comment on art or architecture. The defence might apply to comments on a government policy or criticism of a statement by an individual Minister. Equally it might apply to comment on a court judgement. The defence is generally available in all circumstances where there is an element of public interest.

While it is true that the reputation of an author, artist or architect may be damaged by adverse comments this fact must be balanced against the freedom of the critic to give an honest opinion regarding the worth of the subject under review and against the public interest in reading informed criticism. A further point is that the reading public may make their own judgement on the validity of any comment when presented with the facts upon which the comment is made.

Reviews or comments may be scathing yet, provided certain criteria are met, they will not give rise to liability in defamation. As Lord McLaren stated in *Archer v. Ritchie & Co* (1891): "The expression of an opinion as to a state of facts truly set forth is not actionable, even when that opinion is couched in vituperative or contumelious language".

In order for the defence to apply three criteria have to be met. First, the statement must be a comment on fact. Secondly the facts must be truly stated. Thirdly the facts must concern some matter of public interest. The onus is on the defender to establish these three criteria. Once these criteria have been established the onus then passes to the pursuer to establish that the comment is not fair. Whether or not a comment is fair is determined by its relevance to the facts.

Thus for example, provided a book review does not misrepresent the content of the book, the reviewer is at liberty to state that the book is garbage. This is an opinion on a fact (the content of the book) and as such attracts the defence of fair comment. On the other hand if the reviewer states that the author is illiterate that goes beyond comment on the facts and may indeed be deemed unfair. On reporting a court decision the reporter may set forth the evidence or summarise the case for the prosecution or defence or both and conclude that an acquittal was the wrong result. Despite the fact that such a comment entails imputing criminality to the accused, the defence of fair comment would apply. On the other hand to state that the judge would not recognise a guilty person if he met one in his soup or to accuse the defence of bungling incompetence would go beyond comment on the facts and would render this defence inapplicable.

Privilege
Unlike fair comment the defence of privilege is not generally applicable. The defence of privilege is only available in certain circumstances where the public interest in freedom of speech over-rides any personal interest in reputation.

It is necessary to distinguish between absolute and qualified privilege. Where statements are absolutely privileged they cannot found an action for defamation or verbal injury, even though the statement is motivated by malice or the intent to injure. Where statements are protected by qualified privilege they may give rise to litigation, but the presumption of malice does not operate so the pursuer has the additional burden of proving malice. Malice is difficult to prove and will not be inferred merely from a defamatory statement or imputation. Factors that will assist in establishing malice include the use of particularly harsh or extreme language, prior animosity between the parties or a lack of belief by the defender in the truth of the statement.

Absolute privilege
A successful plea of absolute privilege will render any action in defamation or verbal injury irrelevant. Absolute privilege applies to statements made in the Westminster Parliament whether these are made by MP's or by others, such as witnesses before Select Committees. It also applies to reports and other papers issued under the authority of Parliament including the reports of parliamentary proceedings in Hanford. Absolute privilege also applies to proceedings before the Scottish Parliament and reports and papers authorised by it by virtue of the Scotland Act 1998, s.41.

Judicial proceedings too attract absolute privilege although here the protection afforded is less than in the case of Parliamentary proceedings. Judges enjoy absolute privilege in the exercise of their judicial function. However this privilege may be lost in the event that a judge makes remarks that are not pertinent to the case before the court. This is in contrast to statements made in Parliament where a defamatory statement that has nothing whatsoever to do with the matter under consideration is nonetheless absolutely privileged. It may be noted that Parliament exercises its own discipline. The absolute privilege enjoyed by judges extends to inferior courts and tribunals as well as to supreme courts.

Similarly advocates and solicitors are protected by absolute privilege, not only in respect of what is said in court, but also in respect of written pleadings. Like judges, this protection may be lost where a defamatory statement is made in circumstances that no reasonable person would view as connected with the matter in hand. Witnesses also enjoy absolute privilege in respect of statements made in evidence and also with regard to statements made to the police or in precognition (see for example *Bolam v. Burns* (1994)). Again, privilege is lost where a witness makes statements that are not pertinent to the case. So long as witnesses confine themselves to answering questions put to them by the judge or by counsel absolute privilege applies. In the event that some extraneous comment is made that has no bearing on the question posed then privilege may be lost.

It should be noted that, in contrast to England, parties to civil litigation in Scotland enjoy only qualified privilege. The parties are present for their own benefit and not in the discharge of any public duty. The possibility of an action in defamation or verbal injury may serve to deter frivolous and vexatious litigation. Of course, if a party is called into the witness box by the opposition, the party is a witness and statements are absolutely privileged. The same does not apply in respect of evidence given by the party on his or her own behalf.

Members of juries enjoy absolute privilege. While in theory jurors also could lose absolute privilege by some irrelevant remark there is little scope for such an occurrence and there is no case law on this point.

The protection afforded judicial proceedings extends also to quasi-judicial proceedings and tribunals such as public enquiries, employment appeal tribunals and children's hearings.

It may be noted that absolute privilege has been granted by statute to reports and publications of parliamentary ombudsmen. Furthermore absolute privilege attaches to the Lord Advocate in connection with prosecutions on indictment and in turn to procurators fiscal and advocates depute acting in accordance with the Lord Advocate's instructions. Ministers of the Crown are afforded absolute privilege in the proper exercise of their functions.

Qualified Privilege

While the circumstances giving rise to absolute liability are settled and clear, qualified privilege is relatively fluid in its application. The same statement may attract privilege in one set of circumstances, but not in another. Qualified privilege arises according to the circumstances in which the statement is made rather than being dependent on the status of the person making it or on its nature. Unlike absolute privilege qualified privilege has no role in verbal injury.

Broadly, qualified privilege arises where a statement is made in response to a duty. Anything defamatory that is communicated may be presumed to be a genuine response to the duty rather than evidence of intent to injure. The requirement that malice be averred and proved follows logically.

The duty need not be legal, but may be social or moral. There are circumstances under which citizens will consider themselves under a duty to speak, for example in order to report a suspected crime, or in response to a request for a reference for employment or educational purposes. Equally the press and media in general have a duty to the public to inform. Certain types of reporting are accorded qualified privilege by the Defamation Act 1996, s.15 and Sched. 1. Reports of absolutely privileged proceedings, that is reports of parliamentary and judicial proceedings attract qualified privilege provided the reports are fair and accurate (see for example *Cunningham v. The Scotsman Publications Ltd* (1987)).

Where a statement is made in the belief that there was a duty to make it the court will determine whether there was any such duty. The existence of a duty is a question of law. Where there is no duty the communication will not be privileged. Not only must there be a duty, but the person to whom the communication is made must have a legitimate interest in receiving it.

Consider the following example. I make an allegation to the police that my neighbour is abusing his children. My neighbour sues in defamation. I plead qualified privilege. There is little doubt that I am under a social and moral duty to bring such a concern to the relevant authorities even though, strictly speaking I am under no legal obligation to report crime. The court agrees there is a duty, accordingly my communication is privileged. If my allegation is honestly made my defence succeeds, even though criminal investigation does not find evidence or sufficient evidence to conclude that the children have indeed been abused. If my allegation is malicious then I may well find myself liable in damages. My neighbour may establish malice by proving that I have had insufficient dealings with either himself or his family to form any opinion on whether his children are abused or not. Taken in combination with proof of a long running and acrimonious dispute concerning the height of my leylandii hedge and the fouling of my vegetable patch by his cat he succeeds in proving malice. Had I made the allegation not to the police, but to another neighbour, qualified privilege would not apply. The neighbour would have no legitimate interest in receiving the information.

VERBAL INJURY

The critical differences between defamation and verbal injury may be simply stated. Verbal injury is the appropriate form of action where a reputation has been harmed by words, spoken or written, that are not defamatory. The form of *culpa* that is relevant for liability is malice, but unlike defamation malice is not presumed. Because the statement is not defamatory there is no basis for any such presumption. Therefore malice must be averred and proved. Furthermore a verbal injury is not actionable unless the statement complained of is false. Again, because the statement is not defamatory there is no basis for a presumption of falsity. Accordingly the onus lies on the pursuer to prove that the statement complained of is false.

Verbal injury as distinct from defamation developed out of cases brought by public figures (at least in the local context) such as teachers, ministers and politicians. The basis for complaint was that statements had held them up to public odium, or hatred, contempt and ridicule. The requirements for actionability as outlined in the preceding paragraph were established in 1893 in *Paterson v. Welch* and confirmed more recently in *Steele v. Scottish Daily Record and Sunday Mail Ltd* (1970). Where it can be shown that a false statement was intended to hold the subject up to hatred, contempt and ridicule damages in the form of solatium are available. Likewise any patrimonial loss is recoverable in damages.

Other forms of verbal injury include slander of title, slander of property and slander of business. Slander of title is a false imputation that a person does not own property that he or she is selling. An example of slander of property is a statement that a building is in danger of collapsing as in *Bruce v. JM Smith* (1898). Such a statement would have the effect of reducing the value or selling price of the property. Slander of business might be constituted by a statement that a business is incompetently run or is not in a position to meet its liabilities. It can be seen that in none of these situations is the allegation prima facie defamatory in the sense of lowering the esteem of the victim in the views of right thinking people, nevertheless considerable harm may be done. The nature of the harm done is most likely to be economic and so, provided it can be shown that the statement is false and that the words were calculated to cause pecuniary loss, damages for patrimonial loss will be available. It will not be necessary to prove actual pecuniary loss by virtue of section 3 of the Defamation Act 1952. Since the loss is economic rather than affront, communication of the statement to a third party will be required.

NEGLIGENCE

Finally, the law of negligence may be mobilised where harm is caused by words written without care in circumstances where a duty to the pursuer can be established. This occurred in *Spring v. Guardian Royal Exchange* (1993). In that case the plaintiff who had been employed by the defendants sought employment with other insurers. The reference provided by the defendants contained false and defamatory statements that effectively scuppered the plaintiff's chances of ever working in insurance again. The action was raised in negligence founding on *Hedley Byrne v. Heller & Partners* (1964). The House of Lords treated this as a case of economic loss in which the plaintiff had relied upon the defendants to state facts accurately. It was held by a majority of four to one that there was sufficient proximity between the parties for a duty to arise and there were no policy reasons to deny recovery in damages.

Had the action been raised in defamation the defence of qualified privilege would have applied. References are written in response to a duty and the recipients have a legitimate interest in receiving them. The plaintiff would have been required to prove malice on the part of the defendants and this he could not do. Thus the law of negligence allowed recovery of damages in circumstances where recovery would have been denied under the law of defamation.

---

7. STATUTORY LIABILITY

INTRODUCTION

The other chapters in this book have been concerned primarily with the common law. In this chapter delictual liability arising from statute is briefly considered.

First, requirements relating to statutory negligence in general are outlined. Two sections follow in which particular forms of statutory liability are considered. These are occupiers' liability and liability for animals.

STATUTORY NEGLIGENCE

A claim in negligence may arise in respect of a duty imposed upon the defender by an Act of Parliament. While in such cases it is clearly not necessary to establish the existence of a duty by reference to the neighbourhood principle, proceeding on the basis of statutory duty casts up its own complications.

Where a statute imposes a duty on a party this does not automatically give the pursuer a right to litigate on the basis of the provision. It must be established that the Act contemplates civil liability in the event of breach. In some Acts, it is expressly stated that breach gives rise to civil liability. The Occupiers' Liability (Scotland) Act 1960, s.1 is an example. In other Acts civil liability is specifically excluded, for example by the Health and Safety at Work Act 1974, s.47.

Where the Act is silent on whether civil litigation is to be competent the need for construction arises. Taking into account the whole statute, the pre-existing law, the scope and purpose of the statute and for whose benefit the duty was intended, courts seek to determine the intention of Parliament. This process of construction can be seen in the case of *Cutler v. Wandsworth Stadium Ltd (in liquidation)* (1949). A bookmaker raised an action for damages against a licensed dog track in respect of their refusal to allow him space on their premises to carry on his trade. He founded on the Betting and Lotteries Act 1934, s.11(2) of which imposed on dog track operators a duty to make space available for bookmakers on the track. It was determined in the House of Lords, upholding the decision in the Court of Appeal, that this provision concerned the regulation of the way in which places of amusement were to be managed. Accordingly the provision was intended to benefit the public at large and not bookmakers in particular. While the duty had been breached, this did not entitle the plaintiff to found on s.11 in a civil action.

Where there is doubt regarding whether recourse to civil action is permissible, courts will not allow such action in circumstances where the provision was not clearly intended to benefit the purser. A further example may be found in *Pullar v. Window Clean Ltd* (1956).

Where civil action is competent recovery in damages will only be possible where the loss incurred reflects the harm against which Parliament sought to legislate. A very clear example is provided by the case of *Gorris v. Scott* (1874) in which a statutory duty requiring the shippers of livestock to keep the animals penned in transit was breached. The plaintiff's sheep were swept overboard on voyage. The plaintiff was unable to recover damages since the purpose of the duty was to prevent contagion of disease.

Just as in common law cases it must be shown that the duty was breached and that the loss was caused by the breach. Unlike the common law, in which the standard of care is always the standard of the reasonable man, statute commonly imposes higher standards. Liability may be absolute in the sense that there is no scope for defending a breach, it may be strict in the sense that pursuers are not required to prove fault on the part of defenders. Equally the standard of care may be set at a similar level to the common law. Such is the case in the Occupiers' Liability (Scotland) Act 1960, s.2(1). The standard of care applicable depends on the wording of the statute.

Where a statute imposes absolute liability, evidence of the degree of care taken to avoid the breach will not be relevant in defence. For example, section 22(1) of the Factories Act 1937 provides: "Every hoist or lift shall be of good mechanical construction, sound material and adequate strength, and be properly maintained." In *Millar v. Galashiels Gas Co Ltd* (1949) a workman was killed through the failure of the brake mechanism on a hoist and an action for damages was brought founding on section 22(1). Every possible step had been taken to ensure the proper working and safety of the mechanism. The failure was unexplained and could not have been anticipated. Nevertheless, the House of Lords found the defenders in breach of a duty and therefore liable in damages.

Part 1 of the Consumer Protection Act 1987 imposes strict liability on producers for property damage or personal injury arising from defective products. Consumers may recover compensation without any need to prove negligence or fault on the part of defenders.

Where claims are pursued on the basis of breach of statutory duty the defence *volenti non fit injuria* is in general inapplicable. Of course, where this defence is expressly provided for in the statute it applies. For example, the Occupiers' Liability (Scotland) Act 1960, s.2(3) provides for the application of *volenti*. The defence of contributory negligence is generally available.

THE EXERCISE OF DISCRETION BY PUBLIC BODIES

Ministers of the Crown, local authorities and other government agencies exercise powers under statute. The statutory powers such bodies are given commonly involve the exercise of discretion. Where discretion is exercised carelessly to the detriment of an individual, that person can, in principle seek reparation under the common law. In such a case it is necessary to establish that a duty of care was owed to the pursuer in accordance with the normal common law rules of negligence. There has to be foreseeability of harm, proximity must be established and it has to be fair, just and reasonable before courts will hold that a duty was owed. However, courts are in general reluctant to recognise duties in such circumstances. There is ample scope for courts to decide on policy grounds that a duty of care should be denied. Where administrative decisions have to be made, for example where social workers and others have to decide whether children should be taken into local authority care, or whether a mental patient is to be released into the community, it may be thought that such decisions are sufficiently difficult without the added factor of taking into account potential litigation.

Two types of situation may be identified. First, where a body has discretion on broad policy issues no duty will arise from the way in which that discretion is exercised. So for example, if I suffer food poisoning in a local hotel and attribute this to the fact that the local authority no longer spends sufficient on environmental health, having exercised its discretion to spend more on recreation and amenities instead, this will not be a competent basis for civil action. Even though the hotel has not been subjected to an environmental health inspection, broad policy decisions are not justiciable.

The second type of situation arises where discretion is exercised at an operational level. Principles of administrative law come into play so no liability will arise from the exercise of that discretion unless it is exercised in such an unreasonable fashion that no authority acting reasonably could have exercised discretion in that way. For example the local heath authority prioritises ambulance calls. If I have called for an ambulance for a relative who is suffering chest pain and the available ambulance is directed first to attend a road traffic accident, no liability will arise even though the relative dies from a heart attack and the victims of the road accident turn out to have no more than superficial wounds. The situation might be different if priority is given a fractured radius and ulna over a clear case of myocardial infarction that has been diagnosed by a doctor at the scene. Such a decision would be so unreasonable that civil liability might well arise.

Some care has to be exercised by the courts where public bodies appear to be granted wide immunities. Where claims are struck out (in English cases) or held irrelevant (in Scottish) in the early stages of litigation there is a danger that human rights may be breached. The European Convention on Human Rights, Article 6 states, *inter alia*: "In the determination of his civil rights...everyone is entitled to a fair and public hearing within a reasonable time by an independent and impartial tribunal established by law". This concern arises from the decision of the European Court of Human Rights in *Osman v. United Kingdom* (5 BHRC 293, (1998) *Times*, 5 November, ECHR). Professor Thomson in *Delictual Liability* has suggested that such problems may be avoided by allowing pursuers to lead evidence in proofs before answer, that is before the relevancy of the claim is determined.

OCCUPIERS' LIABILITY

Liability for negligence arising from defective premises or dangers on land is governed by the Occupiers' Liability (Scotland) Act 1960. In fact liability under this statute is not restricted to heritable property, but is extended by section 1(3)(a) to include "any fixed or moveable structure, including any vessel, vehicle or aircraft, and to persons entering thereon". For example if a passenger in your car dies from carbon monoxide poisoning, because the seal on the exhaust manifold leaks and exhaust gasses enter the passenger compartment the case against you would proceed on the basis of the Act.

The Act imposes a duty on occupiers or those having control. This may be the owner, equally the property may be let and the tenant will be the person in occupation. The landlord will not be the person upon whom the duty is imposed unless he or she is responsible under the terms of the lease for maintenance or care of the premises (s.3(1)). If the premises are unoccupied then generally the owner will be subject to the duty since the owner has control. Broadly, the duty lies on the party with effective control. Identification of this party is governed by the common law by virtue of section 1(2).

The duty imposed by the Act is set out in section 2(1). "The care which an occupier of premises is required, by reason of his occupation or control of the premises, to show towards a person entering thereon in respect of dangers which are due to the state of the premises or to anything done or omitted to be done on them and for which the occupier is in law responsible shall, except in so far as he is entitled to and does restrict, modify or exclude by agreement his obligations towards that person, be such care as in all the circumstances of the case is reasonable to see that that person will not suffer injury or damage by reason of any such danger."

It must be noted that liability is not strict, the onus is on the pursuer to establish that the defender was at fault.

The next point to note is that the standard of care imposed is that which is reasonable in the circumstances. The standard depends on the circumstances so the occupier is obliged to go to greater lengths to guard against hidden dangers than against obvious ones since the nature of the danger may be taken into account in determining the standard of care applicable. So far as injury caused by obvious dangers is concerned a pursuer may be deemed to have assented to the risk (s.2(3)). So, for example, there is no duty on a landowner to fence a fast flowing burn. A visitor to the land may be deemed to have assented to the risk if she attempts to cross and is drowned. However this point depends on the type of person who may foreseeably enter the land. If it is foreseeable that very young children will enter the land unaccompanied then this alters the circumstances and the standard of care owed them is greater than it would be in respect of adults.

A duty is owed persons who enter the land or premises and it does not matter whether such persons are entitled to be there or not. Accordingly a duty of care is owed to trespassers. However, the duty may be considered discharged if trespassers have to overcome an obvious hurdle to gain access such as a locked door or high fence. A trespasser cannot break into a lockfast building and then sue under the Act if he is then injured when a rotten floor gives way beneath his feet. On the other hand a trespasser who falls into a bear pit, is caught in a gin trap or mutilated by a landmine will have recourse to the law. For examples of cases involving trespassers and discussion on the way in which the standard of care owed is affected by the age of the pursuer see *McGlone v. British Railways Board* (1966); *Tichener v. British Railways Board* (1984); and *Devlin v. Strathclyde Regional Council* (1993).

A further point to note is that the duty imposed by the Act may be modified or excluded by agreement. Where the premises in question are "business premises" any such modification is subject to the Unfair Contact Terms Act 1977, s.16 of which renders any attempt to exclude or limit liability in respect of personal injury or death void. Other terms are subject to a test of reasonableness. Business (and therefore business premises) is widely defined in section 25(1) and covers government bodies, public authorities and professions as well as manufacturers, retailers and service providers. Contracts allowing persons to enter onto land are expressly covered by the Act (s.15(2)(d) and (e)). In order to be effective to exclude or limit occupiers' liability terms have to be very carefully drafted in accordance with common law rules on the construction of exemption clauses.

Finally, the standard of care imposed by the Occupiers' Liability (Scotland) Act does not detract from or relieve the occupier of liability in respect of any other duty imposed on particular premises or types of premises by any other statute or rule of law (s.2(2)).

LIABILITY FOR ANIMALS

The Animals (Scotland) Act 1987 imposes strict liability, that is liability without any requirement on the pursuer to prove *culpa*, on the keepers of certain animals in certain circumstances. Under the pre-existing common law the keepers of animals *ferae naturae* (of a wild disposition) were presumed to know of the animal's dangerous propensities and were strictly liable for harm resulting from a failure to confine or control the animal. The keepers of animals *mansuetae naturae* (of a gentle disposition) were liable only if it could be proved that either they were aware of the particular animal's dangerous propensities or if they were negligent. The Act supersedes the common law strict liability regime. The old distinction between animals *ferae naturae* and *mansuetae naturae* has become redundant. However, common law actions may still be raised in negligence where harm is caused by animals. The normal rules of negligence apply and the fact that the agent of harm is an animal is largely irrelevant.

Under the Act strict liability attaches to the keeper of the animal as defined in section 5. The keeper is the person who owns the animal or is in possession of it or, where the animal is owned by a child below the age of sixteen, the keeper is the person with actual care and control of the child. The owner remains the keeper of an abandoned animal. Section 3 allows the occupier of land onto which the animal has strayed to detain it. Where this right is exercised the person detaining the animal does not become the keeper.

Strict liability is imposed on the keeper in the event that the animal causes injury or damage (s.1(1)). However not all animals are covered by the Act and not all types of harm or injury caused by those animals give rise to liability under the Act.

Section 1(1)(b) provides that keepers shall be liable if: "the animal belongs to a species whose members generally are by virtue of their physical attributes or habits likely (unless controlled or restrained) to injure severely or kill persons or animals, or damage property to a material extent and (c) the injury or damage complained of is directly referable to such physical attributes or habits.

These provisions operate subject to section 1(4) and (5) so liability under the Act does not arise where either the injury "consists of disease transmitted by means which are unlikely to cause severe injury other than disease" or where injury or damage is caused by "the mere fact that an animal is present on a road or other public place."

This means that a farmer will not be strictly liable if foot and mouth disease spreads from his herd to other animals. Liability will arise where rabies is transmitted through a dog bite since a bite may cause severe injury. Where, as sometimes happens, a cow escapes from a field and causes a motorway pile-up the Act will not apply. On the other hand it is at least arguable that a bull in a china shop will give rise to strict liability since the shop is not a public place. It would have to be established that the damage caused was attributable to the physical attributes or habits of bulls. In situations where liability does not arise under the Act there may be liability at common law, but the pursuer will have to prove negligence or some other form of *culpa*.

Some of the animals covered by the Act are specified. Thus dogs and all animals within the meaning of section 7(4) of the Dangerous Wild Animals Act 1976 are included on the basis that they are deemed likely, in the absence of control or restraint to "injure severely or kill persons or animals by biting or otherwise savaging, attacking or harrying" (s.1(3)(a)). The Schedule of the 1976 Act provides a long list of such animals that includes crocodiles, coral snakes, tigers and wolves. Other animals are listed in the 1987 Act, s.1(3)(b) on the basis that they are likely to cause property damage, particularly to crops, when foraging. The animals thus specified are "cattle, horses, assess, mules, hinnies, sheep, pigs, goats and deer". It must be noted that the absence of a particular animal from any of these statutory lists does not exclude that animal from coverage by the Act. Any animal could be included provided it fits within the definition in section 1(1)(b). However, viruses, bacteria, algae, fungi and protozoa are specifically excluded by virtue of section 7.

Liability imposed by the Act is strict; it is not absolute so there are a number of defences provided for by section 2. No liability arises under the Act if the harm sustained was wholly due to the fault of the victim or the keeper of another animal where that animal is the victim. Furthermore the defence of *volenti non fit injuria* is available in both these circumstances.

As noted under occupiers' liability a duty of care is owed to trespassers. The 1987 Act, s.2(1)(c) provides a defence where a person or animal is injured when trespassing on the keeper's land. In such circumstances, while there may be liability based on fault under the Occupiers' Liability

(Scotland) Act, the keeper is relieved of strict liability under the Animals (Scotland) Act. However, where the animal causing the injury is on the land "wholly or partly for the purposes of protecting persons or property" then the section 2(1)(c) defence is disapplied by section 2(2). Liability will be strict unless the use made of the guard animal was reasonable and if the animal is a guard dog, the use made of the dog must comply with section 1 of the Guard Dogs Act 1975. Compliance with this provision requires guard dogs to be under the control of their handlers or secured so that they cannot roam freely about the premises. Moreover warning notices must be exhibited at every entrance to the premises.

Thus, if I trespass through a field and am gored by a bull, liability will not be strict assuming that the bull has not been placed in the field to act as a guard. I will have to prove negligence or some other form of *culpa* on the part of the defender. If I climb over a garden wall and am mauled by a jaguar, let loose in the garden to act as a guard, then liability will be strict since the use of a jaguar as a guard animal is not reasonable. If I enter a scrapyard and am bitten by a guard dog roaming the premises outwith the control of a handler then liability will be strict. On the other hand if the dog is chained up and there are warning notices at all entrances then I will not recover damages unless I can establish *culpa*.

---

8. NUISANCE

INTRODUCTION

The occupier of heritable property is entitled to enjoyment of his or her land, free from material harm or substantial inconvenience. Broadly put, nuisance arises where one proprietor puts his or her land to harmful use or conducts an activity upon land in unreasonable disregard of the consequences for neighbours. The right of proprietors to use their property in any lawful way must be balanced against the rights of neighbouring proprietors to enjoy their own property. Of course, the law of nuisance applies to the occupiers of property and not solely to proprietors.

This balancing of interests can be expressed as the interplay between two competing maxims. *Qui utitur iure suo neminem laedit* (who exercises a right harms no-one) and *sic utere tuo ut alienum non laedas* (use your property so that you do not harm the property of another).

In the normal case nuisance arises from the use to which the defender has put his or her property, but strictly speaking, "there is no requirement that a nuisance must emanate from the defender's land" (NR Whitty, *Stair Memorial Encyclopaedia*, Vol. 14, para. 2078). Thus, for example, in *Allison v. Stevenson* (1908) an elderly lady encouraged large numbers of pigeons by placing feed for them in the street outside her house. The accumulation of pigeon droppings blocked the pursuers' roans and drainpipes causing material discomfort and property damage. The sheriff (Watson) did consider the lady's interest, she was blind and deaf and feeding pigeons was one of the few remaining pleasures life afforded her, but in view of the measure of harm to the pursuers and the invasion of their interest interdict was awarded.

The modern law of nuisance is focussed on the interest invaded, an interest in property, rather than on the source of the harm. The source need not be use of the defender's own land, but in practice, it usually is. Thus, while the law of nuisance operates to restrict the freedom of proprietors or occupiers to use their land in any way they please, this is an incidental effect of the law and is not of the essence.

The law of nuisance also operates to protect the interest of members of the public in the use and enjoyment of public places including highways or navigable rivers (see Bell, *Principles*, 10th ed. (1899) para. 974). Since, relatively speaking, this interest is more often protected by other means this chapter will concentrate on the invasion of private property interests. In Scotland we do not draw the distinction found in England between public and private nuisance. Rather, we say that nuisance operates to protect two distinct interests, the right to use and enjoy one's property on the one hand and the right to use and enjoy public places on the other.

The primary remedy against nuisance is interdict. Where the court is satisfied that the nuisance caused by the respondent is more than the petitioner can reasonably be expected to tolerate, an order may be made requiring the respondent to discontinue the nuisance. Interdict is not an all or nothing remedy. It does not always entail cessation of the activity complained of altogether. Interdicts may be framed so as to allow continuation of an activity, but not in such a way as to give rise to nuisance.

Where there is reparable loss, for example where an operation has caused material harm to the fabric of the pursuer's building, damages may be sought. In order to raise an action in damages *culpa* on the part of the defender must be established. The requirement of *culpa* in nuisance has long been a controversial issue. For over one hundred years it was possible to argue that liability in nuisance was strict, inasmuch as fault on the part of the defender did not require to be proved. While it is true that nuisance imposes a higher standard of care than is found in negligence, the strict liability view was partly a consequence of the English doctrine of liability for non-natural user and the escape from land of dangerous things, based on *Rylands v. Fletcher* (1868). That issue was settled by the House of Lords in *R.H.M. Bakeries (Scotland) Ltd v. Strathclyde Regional Council* (1985). It is now clearly established that without averments and proof of *culpa*, no damages will be forthcoming. It is also established that *Rylands* is not part of Scots law. However, some difficult issues remain. One area that would benefit from further clarification concerns the relationship between nuisance and negligence.

The interests protected by the law of nuisance are proprietary interests. Accordingly, title to sue is dependent upon a recognised interest in heritable property (*Harvie v. Robertson* (1903); *Dundee DC v. Cook* (1995)). Discomfort and inconvenience are actionable provided it can be established that these are *plus quam tolerabile*, that is more than reasonably tolerable. Material harm is reparable provided *culpa* can be established. It may be that pure economic loss in the form of loss of trade caused by nuisance is recoverable in principle. This issue arose, but was not fully resolved, in *The Globe (Aberdeen) Ltd v. North of Scotland Water Authority* (2000). Personal injury *per se* is not recoverable in nuisance. The appropriate remedy here may be in negligence or under the Occupiers Liability (Scotland) Act 1960. However, where injury to health occurs as a consequence of nuisance, reparation may be available in nuisance along with related losses. In *Chalmers v. Dixon* (1876) the pursuer recovered damages in respect of both harm to crops and the health of his family caused by noxious fumes emitted from a burning heap of pit refuse.

Nuisance is normally, but not always used to describe an activity which is continuing in nature. This explains the status of interdict as the primary remedy. However, it is clear that a remedy in nuisance can be granted against a one-off or isolated occurrence.

Many of the earliest nuisance cases in Scotland concerned interdict against various forms of what can be broadly termed pollution. Examples include smells from the boiling of whale blubber, vibrations caused by machinery and dust from the keeping of chickens. Remedies against many such sources of harm or inconvenience are now provided by statute. The practical advantage of statutory remedies is that they do not always depend upon the individual citizen for mobilisation of the law. The common law continues to operate although in comparison with England the number of cases reaching court is tiny. Recent examples of nuisance actions include: interdicting a "rave"; interdicting floodlights at a tennis club which interfered with fishing; regulation through interdict and damages in respect of the operation of a reservoir which was flooding agricultural land; and damages for failure to make the gable end of a tenement watertight after demolition of part of the building.

ESTABLISHING NUISANCE

A prima facie case in nuisance is established where it can be shown that disturbance or inconvenience exceeds that which is reasonably tolerable. This is expressed as the *plus quam tolerabile* requirement which is a distinctive and characteristic feature of Scots common law nuisance. Citizens are expected to bear lesser degrees of discomfort or inconvenience, *lex non favet votis delicatorum* (the law does not favour the wishes of the fastidious). The issue of whether a particular use of land is *plus quam tolerabile* is seen from the standpoint of the victim (*Watt v. Jamieson* (1954)). Therefore it is not an automatic defence to state that the defender was making only a reasonable use of their land. Rather the question is whether the disturbance or inconvenience is more than the complainer should reasonably be expected to tolerate. Nevertheless, whether an activity is reasonable is one factor that may be taken into account by the courts in balancing the parties' interests. The point is that reasonable use is not of itself decisive. Reasonable use is certainly no defence where the harm complained of is material damage as opposed to substantial inconvenience (*St Helen's Smelting Co v. Tipping* (1865)).

The nature of the locality may be taken into consideration. This was an important factor in a number of nineteenth century cases, for example: *Anderson v. The Aberdeen Agricultural Hall Co Ltd* (1879); *Inglis v. Shotts Iron Co* (1881); *Maguire v. Charles McNeil Ltd* (1922). The reasoning being that the degree of disturbance or inconvenience which proprietors are reasonably expected to tolerate will differ according to whether, for example, the property is situated in an industrial or residential area. During the industrial revolution, when entrepreneurs would set up manufacturing processes, literally in their own back yards, the nature of the locality was a significant consideration. The modern system, whereby land is zoned for industrial or residential purposes under planning regimes, renders the nature of the locality a less vital point than it once was. One cannot now lawfully operate a lime kiln in one's back garden!

The *plus quam tolerabile* requirement was developed in the context of cases brought in respect of intentional nuisance. That is, nuisance created by a deliberate act where harm is known by the defender to be a virtually certain result rather than occurring through negligence, carelessness or inadvertence where there is only a risk (*i.e.* likelihood) of harm. There is a strong argument to the effect that the *plus quam tolerabile* test is inappropriate in cases where nuisance is caused negligently. This is discussed below under "applicability of the *plus quam tolerabile* test".

CULPA

In order to obtain damages the defender must be shown to have been at fault (*R.H.M. Bakeries (Scotland) Ltd v. Strathclyde Regional Council* (1985)). No liability in reparation arises *ex dominio solo* (from ownership or occupation alone) (*Campbell v. Kennedy* (1864)). Arguably, there is an exception to the general rule, that damages depend upon establishing *culpa*, in the case of *Caledonian Railway v. Greenock Magistrates* (1917). This House of Lords case was distinguished in *R.H.M. Bakeries*. It concerns liability for flood damage consequent upon interference with a natural watercourse. This case is generally interpreted as having imposed strict liability on the defenders who were found liable in the absence of fault. However, the unreported opinion of the Lord Ordinary (Dewar) makes it clear that the defenders were found negligent. The opinion of the Lord Ordinary is supported rather than refuted in the House of Lords although their Lordships made no explicit reference to the finding of negligence. It is submitted that this case has been misinterpreted. If so, then no liability in damages without *culpa* is the rule without exception.

The term *culpa* has often been used as a synonym for negligence. However, its classical meaning is broader, the term embraces both intentional and negligent wrongdoing. Classically, *culpa* was contrasted with *dolus* meaning fraud or malice. The current position in Scots law is that *culpa* is a generic term comprising a number of species which include intention, negligence and malice. This generic view of *culpa* has been given authoritative exposition by the Inner House in the case of *Kennedy v. Glenbelle* (1996).

In *Kennedy v. Glenbelle* the occupier of a ground floor tenement flat removed a supporting wall that caused cracking and subsidence in the walls of the higher flats. The affected neighbours sought damages in respect of material harm, basing their case on alternative pleas of negligence and nuisance. The defenders argued that since the averments regarding nuisance were insufficient to support a claim in negligence, the case in nuisance should be dismissed as irrelevant. The Inner House disposed of the argument that negligence was necessary to succeed in nuisance.

The Court determined that while *culpa* was essential, that did not mean that negligence had to be established. Lord President Hope proposed a fivefold model of *culpa*. The species of *culpa* he determined to be: malice, intention, recklessness, conduct causing a special risk of abnormal damage and finally, negligence. These species can be understood as categories of behaviour from which *culpa* may be inferred.

The species require an explanation. Malice is found where the defender intends harm to the pursuer. The defender acts in the certainty, or substantial certainty that the consequence of his or her actions will be harm to the pursuer. In malice there is an additional element of spiteful motive in that the defender seeks to cause harm without benefit to him or herself.

Intentional liability is not limited to consequences that are desired. The defender is culpable, because he or she acts in the knowledge that harm to the pursuer is a certain, or substantially certain consequence of the conduct. Knowledge of the substantial certainty that harm will result is crucial to intentional liability, but it is important to note that knowledge may be constructive. If the defender claims he or she did not actually know that harm would be caused, this will not assist if circumstances dictate that the probability of harm *ought* to have been known.

As the probability of harm decreases *culpa* is characterised in the form of recklessness. Thus, where harmful consequences to the pursuer are highly probable, but less than substantially certain the defender who carries on regardless is reckless. Conduct causing a special risk of abnormal damage, from which fault is implied if the damage results is doubtless, as Lord Hope himself suggests, "just another example of recklessness".

Where the probability of harm decreases further so as to become not a certainty, but a mere risk (or foreseeable likelihood) then *culpa* is framed in terms of negligence.

Culpa may be understood as a continuum, moving from intention, where harm is virtually certain, through recklessness where harm is less than certain but probable to negligence, where there is a mere risk of harm. Malice has an additional element that places it outwith the continuum; thus the classical distinction between *culpa* and *dolus* is preserved. Malice can be understood as intention plus spiteful motive.

In *Kennedy* a relevant averment of *culpa* on the part of the defenders was found in terms of a deliberate act carried out in the knowledge that harm would be the likely result. In short, *culpa* was framed in terms of intention. Arguably *culpa* in such terms is recklessness since Lord Hope spoke of likely results rather than virtual certainties, but it is clear that more than a mere risk of harm was involved.

The lead has been taken from *Kennedy* in subsequent cases and one now finds examples in nuisance actions of *culpa* framed as a deliberate act (or omission) done (or not done) in the knowledge that harm would be the likely result (*GB & AM Anderson v. White* (2000), *Powrie Castle Properties Ltd v. Dundee CC* (2001)). This is a fairly safe route for pleaders to take and is useful for the sake of clarity. By pleading *culpa* in terms of intention or recklessness confusion with the law of negligence is avoided. It also means that the *plus quam tolerabile* requirement is clearly applicable.

APPLICABILITY OF THE *PLUS QUAM TOLERABILE* TEST

According to legal theory, (as discussed in NR Whitty, *Stair Memorial Encyclopaedia*, Vol. 14, paras 2087, 2089 and 2105) the *plus quam tolerabile* test is inapplicable where harm is caused negligently or unintentionally. This is because of the different way the law regards acts that are intentional or reckless and acts or omissions that are merely negligent. With intention the defender knows that harm will result. In negligence the defender ought to foresee a risk that harm may result if sufficient care is not exercised.

Accordingly, where conduct is intentional or reckless and harm follows the only remaining question that needs to be addressed is whether the harm that results is sufficiently grave to amount to a legal wrong. The purpose of the *plus quam tolerabile* test is to answer this question by measuring the gravity of the harm. If the invasion of the pursuer's interest is sufficiently grave to amount to nuisance then a wrong has been done. *Culpa* is inferred so long as it is established that the conduct giving rise to nuisance was intentional or reckless. There need be no discussion on the degree of care exercised by the defender. When conduct is undertaken in the knowledge that harm will result, the fact that care is exercised is irrelevant.

On the other hand, where there is only a risk that harm will result very different considerations apply. The defender is under a duty to exercise care. Culpability arises only if sufficient care is not taken, *i.e.* the standard of care is breached. The defender is under a duty to guard only against risks that are reasonably likely to materialise if sufficient care is not taken and can ignore risks that are remote. The degree of care required is determined by the degree of risk. Risk is measured by multiplying the likelihood of injury by the prospective severity of the harm.

While the purpose of the *plus quam tolerabile* test in intentional nuisance is to determine the gravity of the harm, gravity of harm is taken into account in negligence when risk is measured in order to determine the standard of care applicable. It is not appropriate to take gravity of harm into account again, by applying the *plus quam tolerabile* test. Such duplication is not only unnecessary, it may lead to injustice. For example, where tangible damage is done to property the harm will always be more than reasonably tolerable and therefore liability will arise. This is just, where the materialisation of harm was substantially certain and the activity that caused the harm was conducted regardless. However, where the harm is the materialisation of a remote risk then this is unjust. Under the law of negligence, the defender need not guard against remote risks and ought to avoid liability in such circumstances.

In effect, the *plus quam tolerabile* test imposes a higher standard of care than is found in negligence, in the sense that citizens should take care to avoid altogether conduct that will certainly cause harm amounting to a legal wrong. If the test is applied to determine cases where harm is caused negligently, the effect is to impose a standard of care that is too high. Effectively, liability becomes strict contrary to *R.H.M. Bakeries*.

This may be explained simply. Imagine I make a habit of burning refuse in my back garden. This is within my rights. I do not live in a smokeless zone. I know that smoke will escape from my garden into my neighbours' gardens, but I carry on regardless in the belief that the discomfort or inconvenience to my neighbours will not be sufficiently grave to amount to nuisance. If I burn the occasional pile of leaves in the Autumn or perhaps my Christmas tree and some left over packaging in the Spring then the chances are that while I may cause some annoyance to neighbours, the discomfort they suffer will not be more than reasonably tolerable. If on the other hand, I regularly burn piles of old tyres and the smoke damages the neighbours' wallpaper and soft furnishings then the harm will be found to be more than reasonably tolerable. I will be prima facie liable for nuisance. Enquiry into my culpability will focus on the intentional or reckless nature of my conduct. I might wish to defend myself by arguing that I took care to check that the wind was blowing out to sea when I lit the fire, but this argument will be irrelevant since my act was done deliberately in the knowledge that harm to neighbours would be certain.

Contrast the last example with the following. There is a pile of combustible material in my garden. I do a spot of welding on my car. There is a foreseeable risk that sparks from the welding could ignite the pile and that smoke from the resulting fire could damage my neighbour's property. This in fact is what happens. The focus of the court's enquiry is not on the gravity of the harm caused, but on whether I have exercised sufficient care. I may indeed have been negligent by welding too close to the pile. On the other hand I may have taken all the precautions that a reasonable person would think necessary, yet the fire has started in some unpredictable way. There may, for example, have been a *novus actus interveniens*. Perhaps a stray dog appeared out of nowhere, picked up a welding spark in its coat and ran in a panic into my combustible pile. Perhaps a child, whose presence in the garden was unpredictable, has carried fire from the car to the pile unseen by me as I was underneath the car at the time. In such circumstances the *plus quam tolerabile* test would make me liable, but the law of negligence would not.

In negligence, the fact that harm is caused is not sufficient to make me liable. The harm is not intended. I will only be liable if found negligent and the scope for arguing otherwise may be considerable. In intentional nuisance, the fact that tangible harm has been caused will make me liable provided it is established that my conduct was indeed intentional or reckless. In the case where tangible harm results from a deliberate act done in the knowledge that harm would follow, the scope for arguing against liability is effectively non-existent.

UNINTENTIONAL NUISANCE

Scope for confusion arises where actions are raised in nuisance, but *culpa* is averred in terms of failure to take sufficient care in circumstances where carefulness will avoid harm. In short, where *culpa* is unintentional or negligent. In *Kennedy* Lord Hope stated that: "The essential requirement is that fault or *culpa* must be established. *That may be done by demonstrating negligence, in which case the ordinary principles of the law of negligence will provide an equivalent remedy.* Or it may be done by demonstrating that the defender was at fault in some other respect".

The effect of this statement is arguable. One view is that where nuisance arises unintentionally, the case should be determined according to the law of negligence. This would mean that the action should be raised in negligence and the case should proceed at every point according to the law of negligence. However, it has been argued that in cases of unintentional nuisance it should not be necessary to argue the existence of a duty of care, but the court should go directly to considering whether the standard of care has been breached. The court having first determined that the harm complained of was more than reasonably tolerable.

This view has its attractions. After all, the existence of a duty not to cause harm to neighbours, in the form of an *ex lege* obligation, is of the very essence of nuisance. However, there are some difficulties. The first concerns the view that the *plus quam tolerabile* test applies only in cases of intentional nuisance. The second concerns the recovery of pure economic loss. May the requirement to establish proximity over and above foreseeability of harm be circumvented if the geographical fact of neighbourhood itself can be assumed to impose a duty of care?

These issues can be explored by reference to *The Globe (Aberdeen) Ltd v. North of Scotland Water Authority* (2000).

In that case the pursuers alleged pure economic loss consequent upon nuisance created by road works outside their pub. The operation was conducted in such a way as to make the pavements muddy and unattractive to customers who took their business elsewhere. The pursuers averred *culpa* in terms of the defenders' failure to survey properly the ground before work commenced. In short, *culpa* was framed in terms of a failure to take care, *i.e.* negligence rather than in terms of intention. Work was carried out on a sewer, but on excavation other utilities were discovered underground. The decision was taken to re-route the sewer and consequently the operation took nine months rather than six weeks as originally envisaged. The defenders argued that the loss of custom, as economic loss, was too remote to be recovered.

The pursuers failed at first instance. On appeal the Inner House determined that, while on the basis of the arguments submitted the loss was too remote to be recovered in negligence, recovery in nuisance could not be ruled out. However, no decision on liability could be taken until a prima facie case in nuisance had been made out and so the case was remitted back to the sheriff court for proof before answer.

While it is clear that a prima facie case in nuisance is required before *culpa* is considered this case doesn't comment directly on the applicability of the *plus quam tolerabile* requirement in unintentional nuisance since these words were not used. Perhaps the most significant point to emerge from *The Globe* is that, despite the fact that *culpa* was pled in terms of negligence, the Inner House effectively ruled that the case should be determined according to the law of nuisance rather than negligence. The other major point is that the court were unwilling to infer a duty of care not to cause pure economic loss simply on the basis of neighbourhood.

There is authority to suggest that pure economic loss may be recoverable in nuisance in Scotland provided *culpa* is established (*Laurent v. Lord Advocate* (1860), *Cameron v. Fraser* (1881)). There is also English authority in the form of *Dunton v. Dover DC* (1977). In *Dunton*, a prima facie case was required by the Court. The requirement of a prima facie case in nuisance actions concerning pure economic loss has a clear function. It addresses the issue behind the enhanced requirements of proximity in negligence inasmuch as it serves to restrict the potential field of claimants.

It is a matter of general concern that the law of nuisance should not become a shortcut used to circumvent the requirements of pleadings in negligence. However, it must be noted that nuisance operates within a much more restricted sphere than negligence. So, while "the categories of negligence are never closed", nuisance only arises where there is interference with the enjoyment of heritable property, normally arising from competing use of property. Of course, there will be examples of cases in which negligence and nuisance are advanced as alternative pleas. This is what happened in *Kennedy*.

When seeking damages, the least problematic approach is to frame *culpa* in terms of intention. Where the harm is caused through negligence and it is not possible also to argue on the basis of intention, it is questionable whether the case should be raised in nuisance at all. Although the suggestion from *The Globe* is that the rules of nuisance rather than negligence will apply where the action is raised in nuisance, but *culpa* is framed in terms of negligence, it seems likely that this will remain a contentious issue. It is submitted that nuisance would be considerably more clear were it regarded purely as a delict of intention. It may be that this separation of nuisance from negligence was what Lord Hope intended when he stated that where negligence is demonstrated the law of negligence will provide an equivalent remedy. Currently this is a matter of academic interpretation. Direct judicial comment could provide useful clarification.

In summary, where damages are sought, *culpa* must be pled and proved. Where *culpa* is intentional the court will determine whether any wrong has been done by application of the *plus quam tolerabile* test. The court will balance the interests of the parties by reference to all the facts and circumstances of the case, but in particular must measure the gravity of the harm, discomfort or inconvenience to determine whether nuisance is established. Where *culpa* is unintentional the position is considerably less clear and it may be that the case should proceed according to the law of negligence rather than nuisance. *The Globe* suggests otherwise, but it must be doubted whether *The Globe* is conclusive of the matter.

INTERDICT

Where an activity that gives rise to nuisance is continuing in nature interdict may be sought. There is no requirement on the petitioner to establish fault. However, it must be shown that the harm or inconvenience is more than reasonably tolerable. The determination of this issue will depend upon all the facts and circumstances of the case. Courts have to balance the interests of petitioners against the rights of respondents.

Furthermore, there may be a public interest in the continuation of the activity against which interdict is sought. The Court of Session has an equitable jurisdiction to make a declaratory finding of nuisance, but to suspend operation of the interdict where the public interest in the continuation of the activity outweighs the private interest invaded. Suspension of interdict is intended to allow remedial measures to be taken to abate the nuisance without requiring the cessation of the offensive activity altogether. The power to suspend interdict may be exercised where either: "the granting of immediate interdict would be attended with consequences to the rights of the respondents as injurious, or possible more so, than the wrong that was complained of or ... because the effect of an immediate interdict would be to cause some great and immediate public inconvenience." (*per* Lord McLaren in *Clippens Oil Company v. Edinburgh and District Water Trustees* (1897)) Before the power to suspend interdict is exercised there must first be a finding on the facts (*Ben Nevis Distillery (Fort William) Ltd v. The North British Aluminium Co Ltd* (1948)).

Interdict is available in respect of an existing or anticipated nuisance (*Gavin v. Ayrshire County Council* (1950), *Cumnock and Doon Valley v. Dance Energy Associates* (1992)). In *Webster v. Lord Advocate* (1985) the nuisance complained of was noise from the erection of scaffolding for the Edinburgh Tattoo. *Webster* provides an example of suspension of interdict by the Court of Session. This case also demonstrates that the public interest may be taken into account when balancing the interests of the parties in the process of determining whether an interim interdict may be granted.

Interdict may be sought to put an end to an activity. However, it is important to note that interdicts may be framed in such a way as to allow continuation of the activity, but not in such a way as to give rise to nuisance (*Anderson v. White* (2000)). In this way interdict may be used to regulate an activity and effect abatement of nuisance.

DEFENCES

In general the defender can aim to show that the harm complained of was not more than reasonably tolerable given all the facts and circumstances of the case. The aim in this approach is to establish that on balance, there has been no wrong done.

While it was once a defence to state that the pursuer had come to a pre-existing nuisance (*Duncan v. Earl of Moray* (1809)), this has not been the case since the late nineteenth century (*Fleming v. Hislop* (1886), *Webster v. Lord Advocate*). Accordingly, if a neighbour has tolerated a state of affairs for years, his or her successor in the property will not be barred from legal action.

It is a defence to show that the nuisance was created by third parties for whom the defender is not responsible (*Gourock Rope Works v. Greenock Corporation* (1966)). However, liability may be found in respect of a nuisance created by a third party, but continued by the defender (*Sedleigh-Denfield v. O'Callaghan* (1940)). A further defence is provided if it can be established that harm arose from a *damnum fatale* (act of God) although in Scotland, this would have to be something of the nature of an earthquake or tidal wave, not mere heavy rainfall (*Kerr v. Earl of Orkney* (1857)). Statutory authority for the act complained of also affords a defence (*Allen v. Gulf Oil Refining Ltd* (1981)). The prescriptive period for nuisance is 20 years (Prescription and Limitation (Scotland) Act 1973, s.7(1)).

STATUTORY NUISANCE

Section 79(1) of the Environmental Protection Act 1990 lists statutory nuisances as follows:
(a) any premises in such a state as to be prejudicial to health or a nuisance;
(b) smoke emitted from premises so as to be prejudicial to health or a nuisance;
(c) fumes or gases emitted from premises so as to be prejudicial to health or a nuisance;
(d) any dust, steam, smell or other effluvia arising on industrial trade or business premises so as to be prejudicial to health or a nuisance;
(e) any accumulation or deposit which is prejudicial to health or a nuisance;
(f) any animal kept in such a place or manner as to be prejudicial to health or a nuisance;
(g) noise emitted from premises so as to be prejudicial to health or a nuisance;
(ga) noise that is prejudicial to health or a nuisance and is emitted from or caused by a vehicle, machinery or equipment in a street or in Scotland, road;
(h) any other matter declared by any enactment to be a statutory nuisance.

Many of the situations that once gave rise to common law nuisance actions are now regulated under this provision. One of the key features of the legislation is that mobilisation of the law is carried out by the Local Authority. The authority is under a duty to detect statutory nuisances and, where complaints are brought, to take reasonable steps to investigate. Where statutory nuisance is found, the authority is obliged under section 80 to issue a notice to ensure that the nuisance is abated. Those on whom the abatement notice is served have a right of appeal to the sheriff court. Contravention of an abatement notice constitutes a criminal offence (s.80(4)).

Accordingly, if one suffers discomfort or inconvenience from some source regulated by the Environmental Protection Act it is more simple to complain to the local authority than to embark on the process of seeking interdict through the civil courts. However, the aggrieved citizen is not entirely dependent upon the response of the authority. Section 82 allows for direct application to the sheriff court by individuals.

There are a large number of provisions dotted around statute law which deal with nuisance. However, in this brief treatment one final example will suffice. Imagine you live in a tenement flat and your neighbour practises the electric guitar throughout the night at full volume. This could be the subject of interdict. However, the most straightforward way of dealing with the problem is usually to call the police, on the basis that your neighbour is giving reasonable cause for annoyance. If your neighbour fails to desist, having been ordered to do so by a constable in uniform, he or she will have committed an offence under section 54(1) of the Civil Government (Scotland) Act 1982.

---

9. NOMINATE DELICTS

INTRODUCTION

At the time of Stair the law consisted of a number of distinct delicts. In addition Stair provided a basis from which a general right to reparation based on fault could be developed. In Stair's time this general right was only nascent. The law of negligence developed from this general right. Negligence has become the dominant concern of the modern law yet some nominate delicts survive in the modern context. The archetypal delict of the medieval period, assythment was abolished by statute in 1976. Other delicts, like seduction are technically available, but seldom if ever litigated. Delict can be understood in terms of a general right to reparation based on fault plus a number of distinct nominate delicts, liability for which is also based on fault.

Clearly defamation and nuisance are nominate delicts in the sense that they have names, but they are sufficiently developed and their relevance in the modern context is such that they merit separate treatment in their own chapters. Negligence too is a name, but negligence is not a distinct delict in Scotland in the sense in which it is a tort in England. Negligence in Scots law is tied in with the concept of a general right to reparation based on *damnum injuria datum*.

The delicts considered in this chapter are the nominal delicts of intention. The list of delicts considered is not exhaustive, for example there is no discussion of the Roman quasi-delicts that are sometimes argued to form part of Scots law. A brief outline of the economic delicts is also included.

DELICTS AGAINST THE PERSON

Assault

Assault is both a crime and a civil wrong. Where the perpetrator has been convicted in the criminal courts a compensation order in favour of the victim may be made in terms of the Criminal Injuries Compensation scheme.

Occasionally, where prosecution is not successful a civil action may be pursued. Even though the *mens rea* necessary for criminal conviction is lacking a civil case may yet succeed since liability is established on the balance of probabilities. This is a lesser standard than that applied in the criminal courts where the case must be proved beyond reasonable doubt. Of course, raising a civil action in assault is in no sense dependent upon any criminal proceedings.

The interest protected by the law of assault is physical integrity. The basis for liability is intention. The defender must have intended to invade the physical integrity of the pursuer. The act done must have been deliberate rather than inadvertent or careless. In the latter circumstances an action in negligence would be more appropriate. It is important to note that it is not necessary to establish the intention to harm the victim, only that the harmful act was intentional in the sense of being deliberately carried out. This is made abundantly clear by the case of *Reid v. Mitchell* (1885) in which a farm worker fell from a hay cart as a result of "larking about" by his fellow workers.

The assault complained of must have been without the consent of the victim so complaints of assault are inapplicable, for example in contact sports such as boxing or rugby where the invasion of physical integrity is part and parcel of the game. However, this limitation only applies so long as the rules of the game are adhered to. A boxer might be able to recover in respect of a below-the-belt injury, similarly a hooker who has had his ear bitten off by an opposing prop forward would have an action in delict for assault.

Threatening behaviour falling short of physical contact may amount to assault.

The action may be defended if it can be shown that the defender acted in self-defence or if the assault was the result of an unavoidable accident. As in the criminal law provocation does not provide a defence. Where established provocation may operate as a mitigating factor to reduce any sum awarded in damages.

Seduction

The essence of this delict is that deception or abuse of position has been used to gain a woman's consent to sexual intercourse. This delict therefore contains an element of fraud.

Seduction is seldom if ever litigated nowadays. This is partly a result of changing social mores. The extent to which defloration can be regarded in the modern context as a reparable loss must be limited. So far as pregnancy and childbirth are concerned there are now other legal means by which financial support may be secured, for example through the offices of the Child Support Agency.

In considering reported cases from the nineteenth century it appears that the classic scenario for such a claim to arise was where masters took advantage of the youthful innocence of servant girls in order to lure them into the bedroom. Broken promises to marry also gave rise to delictual actions for seduction. While this delict is technically still operative, it is submitted that its main significance is historical.

Entrapment

Entrapment involves fraudulently inducing a person into a void marriage. Such actions arise occasionally, usually where the marriage is bigamous.

Enticement

This delict involves the unjustifiable enticement of a person away from his or her family. Because enticement must be unjustifiable it follows that this delict may not be founded upon where a child is legally removed from the family for his or her protection or in the best interests of the child. For example, where a child is taken into care by the Local Authority acting in exercise of statutory powers or is legally removed by the police.

Where there is a case in enticement, the other family members may sue for damages in respect of loss of society. Enticement could apply in the case of a husband or wife seduced away from the family by a third party, but there is little evidence of litigation on this basis. It has been suggested that enticement might provide a valid action where a child has been prevailed upon to leave the family to join a sect or cult.

Wrongful detention

The interest protected here is the liberty of the citizen. Nobody can be unlawfully detained against their will. The classic case of damages in respect of wrongful detention is *McKenzie v. Cluny Hill Hydropathic Company* (1908) in which a female guest was detained by the hotel manager in his office for some fifteen minutes. The pursuer was expected to apologise to two other guests whom she was alleged to have slighted. The pursuer successfully recovered damages in respect of the infringement of her liberty and affront.

Such instances of hotel managers taking upon themselves the role of a headmaster are thankfully rare. Complaints of wrongful detention are more likely to arise in connection with police activities. Scope for a successful case of wrongful arrest is limited. So long as police officers act within the law no claim in delict should arise. Where arrest is carried out without warrant, this may be justified on grounds of reasonable suspicion.

In one case where damages were successfully recovered, this was because the actions of the police were found to be unjustifiable. In *Henderson v. Chief Constable of Fife Police* (1988) striking laboratory workers at the Victoria Hospital in Kirkcaldy were taken into police custody. One male pursuer recovered damages because he was unjustifiably handcuffed. A female pursuer recovered damages because she was required to remove her bra. It is not unusual for persons admitted to police cells to be asked to hand over ties or shoelaces in order to prevent them from hanging themselves. However, in this instance, where the pursuer was co-operative and there was no suggestion that she would seek to harm herself, it was held that the removal of her bra constituted an unjustifiable infringement of her liberty.

Harassment

Contravention of lawburrows is an old delict that is technically still competent. Indeed, a small number of twentieth century cases is reported (see for example *Liddle v. Morton* (1996)). Where an individual anticipates harassment, violence or molestation, the delinquent may be called upon to lodge a sum of money known as caution with the court. In the event that lawburrows is contravened, *i.e.* the cautioner harasses or molests the petitioner, the caution is forfeit. Lawburrows is a surviving relic of the period when there was no effective means of criminal law enforcement and the law of delict played a quasi-criminal role in keeping the peace.

Nowadays a person who fears harassment is much more likely to invoke the Protection from Harassment Act 1997. This statute was passed, partly as a response to the phenomenon of "stalking".

The victim may raise an action of harassment seeking damages from the perpetrator. Damages are recoverable both in respect of anxiety and any financial loss. It must be established that there has been harassment amounting to a course of conduct. Damages will not be granted in respect of an isolated event, there must have been harassment on at least two occasions. It must also be established that the defender's conduct was intended to amount to harassment or viewed objectively, may reasonably be interpreted in that way. Harassment is not statutorily defined.

The court may also make a non-harassment order, breach of which is a criminal offence.

Defences to an action of harassment are that the conduct was authorised by law; the conduct was pursued for the purposes of preventing or detecting crime; or the conduct was reasonable in the circumstances.

An article in the Herald on August 28, 2001 suggests a potential issue. The article reported an emerging tendency on the part of parents to employ private detectives to investigate their teenage sons and daughters, primarily to establish whether they take drugs. Clearly the second defence listed above, that the conduct was pursued for the purposes of preventing or detecting crime is intended to apply to the police or customs and excise officers. In the event that a "spied-upon" teenager pursues a non-harassment action against a private detective, it will be interesting to see whether this defence will apply. Will it make any difference if the detective has concerns other than to report illegal drug taking? For example, if the legal sexual and associative habits of the teenager are also the subject of investigation.

DELICTS AGAINST PROPERTY

Trespass

There is a myth that there is no such thing as trespass in Scots Law. This is quite untrue. The point is that in contrast to England, no damages are available for trespass save in respect of damage done.

Historically, the idea of exclusive rights of possession of land did not gain ground until around the end of the seventeenth century by which time much land had been enclosed and land registration was sufficiently reliable.

Litigation arose, primarily from straying domestic animals and the pursuit of game.

Trespass is concerned with temporary and unjustifiable intrusions onto heritable property. Permanent intrusions such as squatting are not trespass, but another delict, intrusion. Intrusion operates where the owner is not in possession at the time. Where the owner is ejected from the property this is yet another delict, ejection. Trespass on moveable property that may be occupied, such as ships or oil rigs is actionable (see *Shipping Co Ltd v. Kurimiawan* (1983) and *Shell UK Ltd v. McGillivray* (1991)).

Heritable property is owned *a coelo usque ad centrum*, that is from the sky to the centre of the earth so air space above the property is protected by the law of trespass. In practice this means that the branches of overhanging trees can be lopped off (*Halkerston v. Wedderburn* (1781)). The law of trespass may not be mobilised against over-flying aircraft by virtue of the Civil Aviation Act 1982, s.2.

While damages are available in respect of tangible harm done, for example to crops, the primary remedy against trespass is interdict. Self-help as a remedy has a practical application in trespass. The landowner may use no more force than reasonably necessary to evict trespassers. Moderate force may be justifiable if the trespasser resists eviction, but too much force may render the landowner liable in assault.

Certain forms of trespass are criminal acts. For example under the Trespass (Scotland) Act 1868, s.3(1) camping on land without permission or lighting a fire is punishable. The Criminal Justice and Public Order Act 1994, Part V creates various offences and gives the police extensive powers to deal with collective forms of trespass. This legislation was passed in order to deal with the perceived mischief created by raves, by hunt saboteurs and by "new age travellers", gathering in large numbers at places like Stonehenge.

Access to land is a thorny issue in Scotland where vast tracts of countryside in the form of estates are owned by a wealthy few, but enjoyed for recreational purposes such as mountaineering, by many. At the time of writing there is a draft Bill about to be laid before the Scottish Parliament. Part I of the Land Reform (Scotland) Bill 2001 provides for a general right to be on land for recreational purposes and to cross land. The Bill details the circumstances under which rights of access do and do not arise and empowers local authorities to regulate access rights and to pass bylaws. The Bill seeks to effect a balance between the "right to roam" and the legitimate interests of landowners. It would be premature to outline in any greater detail the provisions of the Bill since it is regarded as controversial and any legislation that is passed may differ considerably from the Bill as proposed.

Use of land *in aemulationem vicini*
This delict is broadly similar to nuisance although it pre-dates nuisance in Scots law considerably. It means spiteful or malicious use of land with the intention of causing harm to a neighbour. The relevant category of *culpa* is malice.

In order for malice to be inferred it must be clear that the predominant purpose of the activity complained of was to harm or annoy. Therefore if the defender can establish that the offensive act was conducted for his or her own convenience or benefit and that harm to the pursuer was merely consequential, then an action *in aemulationem* will be defeated (see for example *Dewar v. Fraser* (1767)). In such circumstances a claim in nuisance would be more appropriate since nuisance does not require malice.

Examples of cases in which *aemulatio* was successfully pled include *Campbell v. Muir* (1908) and *More v. Boyle* (1967). In the former, petitioner and respondent were neighbouring proprietors on opposite banks of the river Awe. The respondent moored his boat in the middle of the river and cast his rod in such a way as to prevent Sir Robert Usher who had leased the fishing rights from the petitioner, from continuing to fish. Sir Robert had been fishing at that spot for five minutes before the arrival of Muir. The pool where the men were fishing was some 60 yards wide by 146 yards long. Therefore there was plenty of space for Muir to fish the pool without interfering with Sir Robert. The case *in aemulationem* was established.

In *More v. Boyle* the defender severed a water connection in his back garden in order to "get his own back" on neighbours who had refused to pay for a repair on the water pipe. The case *in aemulationem* was held relevant.

Wrongful interference with moveable property

The law of delict in this area is somewhat obscure, particularly since the continuing relevance of the old delict of spuilzie is highly debatable. Bankton described spuilzie as "the violent seizing, or unlawful taking possession of goods from another, without his consent or order of law, for lucre's sake". Originally spuilzie provided a remedy against violent dispossession or theft under which the goods would be restored to their lawful possessor. Spuilzie came also to deal with technical wrongs such as wrongfully withholding goods, for example under a poinding without judicial warrant. Although originating as early as 1318 litigation in spuilzie was at a peak from the fifteenth to the seventeenth centuries.

Twentieth century attempts to revive spuilzie have contributed more confusion than clarity to the law. Examples of cases in which spuilzie has been discussed include: *FC Finance Ltd v. Brown & Son* (1969); *Mercantile Credit Company Ltd v. Townsley* (1971); *Harris v. Abbey National plc* (1997); and *Gemmell v. Bank of Scotland* (1998).

The Scottish Law Commission (Memorandum 31, 1976) suggested that the action of spuilzie was in need of radical reform. They also stated that: "[T]he invocation of ancient remedies of uncertain scope is not necessarily the ideal solution for modern wrongs". Indeed, wrongful interference with moveable property can normally be dealt with by other means, by simple application of the principle of *culpa*, by negligence, by the law of property or by the principles of restitution.

FRAUD AND THE ECONOMIC DELICTS

Fraud

Erskine's definition of fraud is: "a machination or contrivance to deceive" (*Institute*, III, i, 16). Fraud is established where an untrue statement or representation is made or where the statement is believed to be untrue or where the person making the statement is recklessly indifferent whether it be true or false.

Fraud is an intentional delict. It is important to note that the restrictions on recovery of pure economic loss that apply in unintentional or negligent wrongdoing do not apply in intentional delicts. Of course, the form of loss to which fraud is most likely to give rise is economic.

Fraud arises most often in the context of misrepresentation inducing another party to contract. In such circumstances fraud gives rise to both delictual and contractual remedies. For example, in the case of *Smith v. Sim* (1954) the pursuer bought a pub in Montrose relying on turnover figures produced by the defender. The figures turned out to be fraudulent. Under the law of contract Smith had the right to have the contract reduced. The fact that he chose not to exercise this right did not preclude him from recovering damages in delict in respect of fraud.

Passing off

Broadly, passing off is an attempt by a trader to appropriate the goodwill of another trader. This occurs where the name or "get up" of a product is sufficiently similar to another product to amount to a misrepresentation that will confuse consumers. Loss is in the form of reduced sales or damaged reputation.

A fictitious, but clear illustration that may be familiar to readers is found in the Eddie Murphy movie "Coming to America" in which the father of the heroine operates a burger outlet called McDowall's. The "M" is crafted so as to be identical to the "M" used by McDonald's although McDowall maintains that his M is golden arcs as opposed to McDonald's golden arches.

The example shows all the essential elements of passing off as laid down by Lord Diplock in *Erven Warninck BV v. J Townend & Sons (Hull) Ltd* (1979). First, there is a misrepresentation. Second, the misrepresentation is made by a trader in the course of trade. Third, the misrepresentation is made to prospective customers of his or ultimate consumers of goods and services provided by him. Fourth, the misrepresentation is calculated to injure the business or goodwill of another trader. Fifth, the misrepresentation has caused or probably will cause damage to the business or goodwill of the other trader.

In our example it is probable that McDowall sought to benefit from McDonald's goodwill. His motivation was to benefit himself rather than to harm McDonald's. However he cannot evade liability on this basis. If harm to McDonald's is reasonably foreseeable then the requirements for liability can be satisfied. Harm to McDonald's arises, either because customers go to

McDowall's in the mistaken belief that they are eating at McDonald's or because, having eaten at McDowall's they foreswear burgers for life!

The primary remedy in cases of passing off is interdict. Damages may also be available although the process of quantifying loss may present problems.

Breach of confidence

It is a delict to publish or otherwise disseminate information provided in confidence or information gained from a relationship of confidence. In the commercial context trade secrets may be protected by the law of contract. Restrictive covenants forbidding divulgence of sensitive business information are enforceable to the extent that they are reasonably necessary.

However breach of confidence is not restricted to the commercial context. An obligation to maintain confidentiality may arise in circumstances as diverse as employment in the secret service where divulgence of information might threaten national security on the one hand and between married partners or even lovers on the other. An obligation of confidentiality clearly arises between banker and client, solicitor and client or between doctor and patient. The obligation arises wherever there is a relationship of confidence irrespective of whether there is a contractual relationship.

Both parties to the relationship are bound by the obligation. The obligation also extends to any third party to whom one of the parties has divulged information. Thus if the editor of a newspaper publishes information that is known to be confidential or that a reasonable person would know should be confidential in the circumstances then liability in delict will arise (see *Lord Advocate v. Scotsman Publications Ltd* (1988)).

The primary remedy is interdict to prevent dissemination of information. Damages may be recoverable although depending on the circumstances damages may be difficult to assess. In the "spycatcher" case, *Attorney-General v. Times Newspapers* (1988) the editor of the Sunday Times was liable to account for profits following publication of confidential information.

Inducing / procuring breach of contract

It is an actionable delict if a person induces another to breach a contract to which he or she is party. This is a relatively recent delict recognised by Sots law in the case of *British Motor Trade Association v. Gray* (1951). Inducing a breach of contract is a wrong in itself. In order to be actionable the means used does not have to be unlawful. The innocent party to the contract can sue the party who induces the breach in delict. Of course, he or she may also sue the other party to the contract for breach. Before damages can be awarded there must be loss. However, where breach has been induced courts will have little difficulty in inferring loss. Scottish courts require knowledge of the contract before a person can be held liable for inducing breach. The strong suggestion from the case of *Rossleigh Ltd v. Leader Cars Ltd* (1987) is that actual knowledge of the existence of a contract is required although the specific terms of the contract need not be known.

Inducing breach of contract deals with the situation where the delinquent is able to prevail on one party to the contract, perhaps by threats, perhaps by financial inducement to breach. Procurement refers to the situation where the delinquent is able to engineer a breach of contract where the party is unwilling to breach. This can be done directly, for example by vandalising machinery essential to performance of the contract or indirectly, for example by inducing a breach of contract on the part of a supplier. In contrast to inducing breach of contract, liability only arises in respect of procurement where unlawful means are used to procure the breach.

Wrongful interference with performance of contract
This arises as an actionable wrong where a third party interferes with a contract in a way which falls short of producing a technical breach. This is a development on the delict of inducing breach arising from the case of *Torquay Hotel Co Ltd v. Cousins* (1969). Direct interference will give rise to liability whether or not unlawful means are used. Indirect interference will only give rise to liability where unlawful means are employed.

Wrongful interference with trade
It has been argued that economic delicts such as wrongful interference with contract and inducing and procuring breach should be subsumed under the broader heading of wrongful interference with trade. This approach derives from the English case of *Lonrho plc v. Fayed* (1990) and is to some extent supported in Scots law by *Shell UK Ltd v. McGillivray* (1991). The requirements of this new delict call for intention to harm and actual loss caused by unlawful means.

Intimidation
This delict derives from the House of Lords case of *Rookes v. Barnard* (1964). It arises where one party threatens a second with an unlawful act unless the second party causes economic harm to a third party. In *Rookes* three trade union officials threatened their employer, BOAC with unlawful strike action unless Rookes' employment was terminated. Rookes succeeded in his case against the three officials.

Conspiracy
The delict of conspiracy requires a combination of parties acting together to cause economic harm to another party. If parties act together with the predominant motive of causing harm to another then liability in delict arises whether or not the means used to inflict harm are unlawful.

Thus while it is not an actionable delict for a business to attempt to drive another concern out of business, for example by undercutting prices (see *Allen v. Flood* (1898)) where two or more business or parties combine with the intention of causing economic harm then delictual liability arises. So a course of action that would not be delictual if carried out by a single party becomes delictual by virtue of conspiracy. Where the means used are lawful and the predominant motive behind any course of action is to benefit the participating parties and intention to cause harm to the pursuer is absent then no delict is committed. This follows from *Crofter Hand Woven Harris Tweed*

Co Ltd v. Veitch (1942). The onus is on the pursuer to establish predominant motive to harm. The pursuer must also establish economic loss. Where the means used are unlawful, in the sense of being criminal, in breach of contract, in breach of statute or delictual, then the pursuer has to establish that the conspirators intended harm. He or she does not have to show that harm was the predominant motive for the acts.

---

10. REMEDIES

INTRODUCTION

Generally where loss is caused by a wrong, the law provides a remedy. Where the loss is quantifiable in money terms the remedy sought will usually be damages. However, depending on the circumstances, other remedies may be more appropriate.

The simplest remedy is self- help. Clearly the scope of self-help is limited. Its most clear application is in trespass. A landowner may construct a fence or dyke to keep other people or animals from straying onto his or her property. Equally, reasonable force may be used to eject trespassers from premises or land. Trees or shrubs that encroach on land, for example branches that overhang one's property, may be lopped or pruned with no right of recourse accruing to the owner.

A person who has been wronged may seek declarator. A declarator is given when a state of affairs amounting to a delict is found to exist. For example, a declarator may provide that a state of affairs amounts to a nuisance. Normally an action for declarator will be accompanied by a plea for damages or interdict since the award of declarator itself does not compel the defender to do anything, to refrain from doing anything or to pay anything. It is simply a statement of the legal position of the parties.

The principal remedies are interdict and damages. These are both complicated and entire books have been devoted to consideration of each. The following text is an outline guide to the essential points only.

INTERDICT

The essence of interdict is that prevention is better than cure. Interdict is sought to prevent an anticipated wrong or to put an end to a continuing wrong. An interdict restrains the activities of the party against whom it is awarded. In short, it forbids the party interdicted from conducting the activity specified. If the terms of the interdict are breached, the party in breach will be liable to a fine or imprisonment. The party seeking the interdict is the petitioner. The party against whom the interdict is sought is the respondent.

Interdict is broadly equivalent to the English remedy of injunction. The use of the term injunction is inappropriate in Scotland. Beware of loose usage by newsreaders and suchlike. When an injunction is awarded by the English courts, for example against publication or distribution of memoirs in breach of the Official Secrets Act, it has proved necessary to seek separately, an interdict in the Court of Session, so that the Scottish media also is restrained from publication.

Interdict has no real application in negligence. Interdict is an appropriate remedy in delicts of intention, for example in defamation, trespass, nuisance and use of land *in aemulationem vicini*. Interdict is used to protect intellectual property rights and is generally applicable in the economic delicts such as passing off or wrongful interference with contracts.

Interdicts must be framed in clear and precise terms so that the party interdicted should be left in no doubt regarding the forbidden activity. The terms of the interdict must be no wider than necessary to curb the wrong complained of.

Interdicts may be permanent, that is made without limit of time, or interim. An interim interdict is an immediate remedy that may be applied for at any stage in the process of application for a permanent interdict. For example, if an interdict is sought to prevent publication of defamatory material in a newspaper an interim interdict may be required if intended publication is imminent. The award of a permanent interdict requires more time and justification and will not help the petitioner if the material is published before the court reaches a conclusion. The interim interdict serves the purpose of preventing publication while the more detailed consideration required for permanent interdict takes place.

Interim interdicts are awarded at the court's discretion. There must be a prima facie case, in other words on the basis of the petitioner's pleadings it must appear that a relevant case in defamation, or nuisance or whatever wrong is complained of has been made out. The court will then consider the balance of convenience between the parties. For example, it may be argued that the award of interdict will cause a greater wrong to the respondent than the wrong complained of by the petitioner. Any public interest in the activity complained of will be taken into account by the court. Only where the balance of convenience is held to be in the petitioner's favour will interim interdict be granted. An interim interdict is valid until recalled by the court.

In general interdict is only awarded where there is a genuine prospect of future wrongs. Interdict is not competent in respect of an activity that is unlikely to be repeated.

DAMAGES

The purpose of damages is to repair the loss suffered by the pursuer. Damages in Scots law are not intended to penalise and do not reflect the degree of culpability of the delinquent party. In awarding damages the courts seek, insofar as is possible, to effect *restitutio in integrum*. That is, to restore the pursuer to the position he or she would have been in had the delict not occurred.

Broadly, claims for damages fall under two heads, solatium, and patrimonial loss. Solatium is awarded in respect of pain and suffering. This includes affront or injury to feelings caused by defamation. The expression "patrimonial" derives from the Roman concept of *patrimonium* meaning a person's estate. Patrimonial loss covers all tangible economic losses including property damage and financial harm.

Where the harm sustained is property damage the process of assessing the quantum (amount) of damages is relatively straightforward. The pursuer may recover from the defender the cost of repairing or replacing the property. There may be derivative losses that are also recoverable in damages, so if a car is damaged through negligence the defender may be held liable to pay the costs of a hire car while the original vehicle is being fixed.

Damages in personal injury cases

Where the pursuer has suffered personal injury the claim for damages in respect of pain and suffering will be under the head of solatium and any derivative losses will be claimed under the head of patrimonial loss.

Placing a monetary value on pain and suffering is an inexact science. The severity and nature of the injuries will be taken into account along with the extent of any disability or loss of amenity. Awareness of pain is relevant, so if the pursuer is in a coma there may be no award of solatium. Anything which reduces the pursuer's enjoyment of life, including pain and suffering caused by the realisation of reduced life expectancy will be taken into consideration. In practice, close regard is paid to the sums awarded in previous decisions and lawyers make great use of McEwan and Paton's loose leaf guide. By using this guide it is possible to find out recent awards made in respect of particular injuries. For example, if a client has lost a leg the guide will give details of sums awarded in previous instances of the same injury.

Solatium may be awarded not only in respect of pain and suffering from the date of injury to the date of proof, but also in respect of future pain and suffering where this is relevant. Where the victim has died, immediate relatives may claim in respect of: distress and anxiety caused by the victim's suffering while still alive; grief and sorrow caused by death; and loss of the victim's society.

Damages in respect of patrimonial loss cover loss of earnings, outlays and reasonable expenses. A sum may be awarded in respect of necessary services rendered by relatives under the Administration of Justice Act 1982, s.8. Section 9 of the same Act provides that a sum may be awarded to relatives in respect of services that the victim is no longer able, on account of his or her injuries, to render the family. This would include such things as vehicle maintenance, childcare and housework. Where the victim has died, relatives may also recover damages in respect of loss of support and funeral expenses.

Patrimonial loss is subdivided under two further heads, past and future of which future loss is both the most important and most difficult to calculate. The pursuer may claim for loss of earnings up until the date of proof. The sum payable is net wages or salary. To calculate future earnings the net wage at the date of proof is taken as the multiplicand. The court must determine the number of years over which damages are due in respect of future earnings. This is the multiplier. The multiplier is never as great as the number of years the pursuer has left until retirement. The product of the multiplicand and multiplier is then calculated to give a lump sum that can then be invested.

Expenses such as the cost of nursing care can be taken into account under future losses.

Awards of damages, both past and future are subject to the payment of interest.

Deductions

Damages in respect of patrimonial loss are subject to deductions. Earnings or remuneration from an employer, unemployment benefits prior to the date of the award of damages and any benevolent payment made by the person responsible for the injury should all be taken into account in reducing the award of damages.

Under the Social Security (Recovery of Benefits) Act 1997 various social security benefits paid to the defender during the "relevant period" must be deducted from the sum payable to the pursuer by the person against whom the award has been made, the compensator. The "relevant period" is five years from the date of the accident or five years from first claiming benefit in respect of "a disease". Where damages are paid within five years of the accident, the relevant period ends at the date of payment. The sum deducted by the compensator from the victim's compensation is then paid directly to the Secretary of State.

Provisional Damages

Where it is proved or admitted that there is a risk that the pursuer's health or condition will seriously deteriorate in the future the Administration of Justice Act 1982, s.12 provides that a provisional award of damages may be made. Such an award is only permissible where the defender is a public authority or is insured. A provisional award of damages means that the pursuer may seek further damages in future if the risk of serious deterioration materialises. At that stage it will be possible to assess the extent of pain and suffering or any reasonable expenses. It is within the discretion of the court to set a time limit against future claims.

Interim Damages

The court may grant an award of interim damages before the process of litigation is concluded. Interim payments will only be awarded where liability is admitted by the defender or where there appears no question that the pursuer will succeed. This means also that there should no prospect of a substantial reduction of damages on grounds of contributory negligence.

APPENDIX: SAMPLE EXAMINATION QUESTIONS AND ANSWER PLANS

1. Senga McGlumpher asks her building society to instruct a surveyor to conduct a detailed structural survey on a house that she is considering buying. The building society instructs a firm of surveyors, Bobbit & Co to conduct a full structural survey on behalf of a Ms McGlumpher. The survey is conducted and the report concludes that the building is sound.

It transpires that Senga cannot afford to increase her mortgage. However her sister Edna is interested in the property and Senga gives Edna the survey on condition that Edna pay the surveyor's invoice. Edna settles the bill. In reliance on the survey Edna buys the house. The house turns out to suffer badly from rising damp that will cost £10,000 to put right. Edna contacts Bobbit & Co who appear willing to discuss compensation with her.

Advise Bobbit & Co.

Notes for answer

There is a defect in the quality of Edna's house. She has suffered pure economic loss. Ought Bobbit & Co to compensate her? This issue has to be determined according to the principles of *Hedley-Byrne v. Heller*. Can the requirements of proximity be satisfied? In circumstances of a full structural survey you can presume that there has been an assumption of responsibility on the part of Bobbit & Co. If you want to impress the examiner by a brief but relevant foray into the law of contract you may note that while it is possible to avoid liability by use of a contractual term, where a full structural survey has been instructed it is unlikely that a court would uphold any such term as reasonable within the meaning of the Unfair Contract Terms Act 1977. There is no mention of any such term or disclaimer of responsibility in the text so an answer that does not consider the issue is fine, but there should be some mention of assumption of responsibility since that is a *Hedley-Byrne* requirement.

Edna appears to have relied on the exercise of due care by Bobbit & Co and since they are surveyors her reliance is reasonable. The problem bears a superficial resemblance to *Martin v. Bell Ingram* in which the pursuer did recover damages in respect of a negligently conducted survey, but there is an important distinguishing feature here that you should spot. Our case is distinguishable on the basis that the party who relied upon the survey was not the person on whose behalf the survey was conducted. The particular transaction was the same, the purchase of the house that was the subject of the survey, but the identity of Edna was unknown to Bobbit & Co. Therefore Edna's case falls foul of *Caparo v. Dickman*. To be liable Bobbit would have to have known that Edna herself would rely on their survey. The relationship between Edna and Bobbit & Co is insufficiently proximate for a duty of care to avoid causing pure economic loss to arise.

Apparently Bobbit & Co do not realise that the Ms McGlumpher who is seeking compensation is not the Ms McGlumpher upon whose behalf the survey was conducted. The fact that Edna has settled Senga's bill is irrelevant. Edna has fulfilled Senga's contractual obligation, but this does not mean that Bobbit & Co owe Edna any obligation in delict. You have been asked to advise Bobbit & Co. Forget any sympathy you may have with the unfortunate Edna and act like a professional. Advise Bobbit & Co that they are not obliged to compensate Edna. If, as a matter of commercial practice, they decide to compensate Edna to some extent that is up to them. The point is that they are under no obligation.

2. Bill is the manager of a foundry. He hears cries and a commotion coming from a part of the foundry one hundred metres away. When he goes to investigate he discovers that there has been a spillage of molten metal and sees two men wrapping a third in a fire blanket. He can see that the victim's clothes are burning. He does not recognise the victim since his face is badly burnt and his hair has gone. He is screaming. At that point a crucible fractures and Bill and the two helpers spring away. The eruption of molten metal engulfs the original victim who burns to death. It dawns on Bill that the victim is his brother in law. As a result of the incident Bill suffers clinical depression and insomnia. When he does sleep nightmares awaken him.

The Foundry owners admit that the incident occurred as a result of their negligence, but they deny that they owed Bill a duty of care in respect of psychiatric harm. Can Bill recover damages?

Notes for answer
Clearly Bill has suffered loss in the form of a recognised psychiatric illness so the requirements of *Simpson v. ICI* are satisfied. The issue here is whether Bill should sue as a primary or a secondary victim. Since both appear possible from the text you should consider both possibilities and evaluate Bill's chances of recovering damages in each.

Applying *Page v. Smith* Bill can recover damages as a primary victim provided he was within the area of potential harm. The fact that he incurred no physical injury is irrelevant since it is clear that provided a duty not to cause physical harm is breached the victim can recover damages even though the harm that results is psychiatric.

You might like to illustrate the application of *Page v. Smith* and the importance attached to being in physical danger by reference to *White v. Chief Constable of West Yorkshire*, *Hale v. London Underground*, *Young v. Charles Church* and *Hunter v. British Coal*. However there are potential pitfalls. It is critical that you cite *Page v. Smith* in your answer since that is the source of the rule that you are applying. The other cases largely serve to illustrate the application of that rule. Failing *Page v. Smith* the next best case upon which to base your answer is *White* since that too is a decision of the House of Lords. The question every student wants and no examiner ever sets is "Write all you know about ... (*e.g.* the recovery of damages for psychiatric harm in negligence)." If you solve the problem identifying and applying the appropriate rule and preferably the correct source of the rule then you will do fine. If you can embellish your answer by a broader discussion of the case law that is clearly related to the issues raised by the problem then so much the better.

Whether Bill can recover as a primary victim will depend upon his ability to establish that he was within the area of potential danger when the second spillage occurred. The text appears to suggest that he was.

In order to recover as a secondary victim Bill will have to satisfy the requirements set out in *Alcock v. Chief Constable of South Yorkshire*. Clearly Bill was present during the second incident and witnessed the immediate aftermath of the first with his own senses. Bill must establish close ties of love and affection with his brother in law and he will have to lead evidence to prove this. You do not know whether Bill will be able to prove this or not, but you might conclude that the requirement of a close tie of love and affection presents a barrier to recovery as a secondary victim that does not apply to Bill's case as a primary victim. If Bill cannot prove close ties of love and affection to the satisfaction of the court then he may still recover damages as a primary victim provided the court is satisfied that he was within the area of potential danger.

3. Horace is travelling by train. The train is crowded and Horace has to stand by the door. There is a notice above the door warning passengers that it is dangerous to lean against the door or out of the window while the train is in motion. The door locks are controlled by a master switch in the driver's compartment. When the train leaves the station Bob, the driver, forgets to flick the switch. Bob's train is running late and he drives much faster than usual in order to make up time. When travelling fast round a bend the standing passengers are thrown outwards. Most have found something to hold onto, but a large man standing in front of Horace has found no support and he is thrown against Horace. The door opens and Horace falls onto the track. Horace's spine is severed at the neck, but he is not dead. The door slams shut as the train immediately enters a bend in the other direction and nobody realises Horace is gone so nobody pulls the communication cord to stop the train.

A thief sees Horace and rifles his pockets. He takes Horace's wallet and proceeds fraudulently to use Horace's credit cards. Debts of several thousand pounds are incurred. This loss is not covered by any card protection plan or other insurance. The credit card companies are entitled under contract to hold Horace liable for these debts. The thief is never caught.

Finally Horace is taken to hospital. He lives, but is paraplegic. His career as a solicitor is at an end. He is no longer able to do odd jobs around the house or to cook for his family, a task which has generally fallen to him in the past since he enjoys cooking and his wife does not. These tasks are now performed by his father who also provides nursing care.

You are asked to advise Horace regarding the possibility of recovering his losses. You also need to advise him of possible defences against his claim.

Notes for answer

A question of this nature involves several issues. You are being assessed, not only on your knowledge of the law, but on your ability to provide an analysis. Take time to read the text carefully and plan a structured answer around the issues that arise. The first task is to identify the issues and it may be a good idea to set these out in an introductory paragraph before examining the issues in turn.

Clearly the problem involves negligence. In any problem involving negligence you should consider the existence of a duty of care, the standard of care applicable, whether the duty was breached, causation and remoteness of damage. You need not give each of these aspects equal weight. In this problem the existence of a duty, the standard of care and breach are pretty straightforward. More detailed consideration has to be given the issues of causation and remoteness of damage. The text also raises the issue of vicarious liability. In addition, because the text provides some detail on the types of loss suffered by the victim you should consider what may be claimed under different heads of damages. Finally, you will need to consider possible defences to the action since you have been asked to do so.

Horace may be advised to raise an action in negligence against the railway company. It is clear that the negligent act or omission occurred in the course of Bob's employment. Therefore his employers will be vicariously liable. Authority on this point may be cited such as *Kirby v. N.C.B.* The point is simple and there is no difficulty in applying the general rule so there should be no need to embark on a lengthy discussion of the case law. Horace may elect to sue Bob either instead of or as well as the railway company. Liability is joint and several. In practice Horace would probably name both as defenders in his action, but would have more hope of recovering damages from the railway company than from Bob.

There can be no doubt that a duty of care is owed Horace by Bob since passengers on a train are within the reasonable contemplation of the driver as being likely to be affected by his acts or omissions. This is a straightforward application of the neighbourhood principle in *Donoghue v. Stevenson*. There will be no difficulty in establishing proximity. The existence of a duty is fairly obvious so there is no need to dwell upon it at length. Horace should have no difficulty in establishing breach of the standard of care since Bob has neglected to follow normal practice in implementing a safety system that is found in all modern trains in this country. Bob has made a negligent omission. Bob may also have been negligent or possibly reckless in driving a crowded train so fast. You can't tell from the text whether his speed was excessive in terms of the margins of safety for the particular section of track. However the clear implication to be drawn from the text is that Bob was driving too fast.

Horace should be able to establish that an accident of the type he has suffered, *i.e.* falling out of the door, was a reasonably foreseeable consequence of Bob's failure to lock the doors, particularly in circumstances where a fast moving train is crowded to the extent that passengers are standing in the space between carriages. Certainly it is foreseeable that standing passengers will be thrown outwards when a train is driven fast round a corner. This is the effect of centrifugal force, but you are not being examined on physics! Having considered the cases of *Muir v. Glasgow Corporation* and *Hughes v. Lord Advocate* you can conclude that the requirements of foreseeability of harm are satisfied since an accident of this type was a foreseeable likelihood.

Horace will have to establish that his losses are directly attributable to Bob's negligence. Horace has suffered two forms of loss. He has incurred personal injury and losses arising from personal injury on one hand and the loss of his wallet and consequent financial loss on the other. You need to consider these losses separately. Deal with personal injury first.

Bob's negligence is the *causa sine qua non* of Horace's accident. Is it also the *causa causans*? The defenders may seek to argue that the direct and immediate cause of Horace falling out the door was the large man whose actions amounted to a *novus actus interveniens* breaking the chain of causation between the original negligent omission and the accident. You should identify and evaluate this potential argument.

A court would be unlikely to regard the action of the large man as a *novus actus interveniens*. This is because his loss of balance was an involuntary act caused by the movement of the train which was being driven too fast. The man's loss of balance was a reasonably foreseeable consequence of the motion of the train that was under Bob's control. Therefore the large man was an unwitting agent of Bob's negligence and not an independent actor. For this reason he cannot be held to have broken the causal chain between Bob's negligence and Horace's accident. Accordingly Bob's negligence is the *causa causans* of Horace's injuries.

This may be a good point at which to consider the other loss, that is the loss arising from the theft of Horace's wallet. Since there is no prospect of recovering from the thief it must be considered whether this loss too can be recovered from Bob and the railway company. There are a number of reasons for answering this question in the negative. First, loss of this nature is not foreseeable as a reasonable and probable consequence of Bob's negligence so this claim should fall on the application of *Muir v. Glasgow Corporation*. Indeed this loss is too remote. This claim also fails on causation. While Bob's negligence is the *causa sine qua non*, since but for it Horace would not have been lying injured in a place where he could be robbed, it is not the *causa causans* since the theft amounts to a *novus actus interveniens* breaking the causal link between Bob and the loss. The theft is a *novus actus interveniens*, because it is the independent act of a third party unconnected in any way with the original negligence. In this case the loss lies where it falls. In the circumstances it is possible that the credit companies may be persuaded to write off the debt.

Horace may be advised to seek solatium in respect of his pain, suffering, loss of amenity and any contemplation of loss of life expectancy. He would be able to recover damages in respect of services now provided by his father under the Administration of Justice (Scotland) Act, ss.8 and 9. Furthermore he would be able to recover damages in respect of loss of earnings. Since you are not provided with Horace's earnings in the text you may safely assume that you are not required to calculate a sum. To be on the safe side you might note that Horace's salary at the date of proof (the multiplicand) will be multiplied by a notional figure representing the years Horace had left to work, although the latter figure (the multiplier) will not be as great as the number of years until Horace was due to retire.

Horace is likely to succeed in his claim. There should be no reduction in damages for contributory negligence since there is nothing in the text to suggest that Hamish contributed to his own injuries. Equally the defence of *volenti non fit injuria* will not succeed. While the notice warned of the dangers of leaning on the door, Hamish was not leaning on it, he was pushed against it. There is nothing to suggest that in getting on the train he consented to assume the risk that Bob would drive negligently.

4. Maybeline and Nadine work for a firm of accountants. Maybeline feels bullied and harassed by one of the partners, Gloria, because Gloria behaves towards her in an utterly unreasonable fashion. The firm operate a grievance procedure. Maybeline fears that making a complaint will get her into more trouble. Nadine enters a complaint stating that Gloria is overbearing, rude and impatient and that she bullies Maybeline. On Friday night in the pub Maybeline spends most of the evening bitching about Gloria to anyone who will listen. As the evening wears on the tales become grossly exaggerated and Maybeline makes various unfounded allegations about Gloria's slapdash approach to her work for clients in front of the local inspector of taxes.

The senior partner has a word with Gloria about the complaint made against her and word reaches her ears of the discussions in the pub. She intends suing both Maybeline and Nadine for damages in defamation. Will she be successful?

Notes for answer

The case against Maybeline appears clear. It appears that Maybeline has made false statements casting doubt upon Gloria's professional competence. Such allegations are generally accepted as defamatory so there should be little difficulty in establishing that what has been said about Gloria would lower her in the esteem of right thinking people, having applied Lord Atkin's dictum in *Sim v. Stretch*. Because the statements are false, intention on the part of Maybeline will be presumed.

Any case against Nadine is most unlikely to succeed. For one thing it is arguable whether the allegations she made against Gloria would amount to defamation if they were false. The comments were not pleasant, but could they bear a defamatory meaning? This is for you to consider and decide, but there is no obviously right answer. In any case the comments cannot satisfy the test for defamation since it appears from the text that nothing but the truth was communicated and a defamatory statement is by definition false. Truth (*veritas*) affords a complete defence. Moreover, having followed the correct procedure for raising complaints Nadine's comments attract the protection of qualified privilege. It may be easily inferred that Nadine made the complaint considering herself under a duty to do so. Since the grievance procedure was followed the comments would have been made to a person with an interest in hearing them. Certainly a senior partner has a legitimate interest in being told of serious difficulties in office relationships. All these factors point to the conclusion that Nadine's comments enjoy qualified privilege. Had the allegations been false and defamatory Gloria could not recover damages from Nadine in a defamation action unless she proved malice on Nadine's part. Since the allegations are true there is no case in defamation.

5. *Hilda moves into a new house. Her next door neighbour is Stan. Stan has been a keen pigeon fancier since he retired 10 years ago. Stan is widowed, he has no family and pigeons are his only pleasure. Hilda does not like birds and she has a particular antipathy towards pigeons. Hilda complains often to Stan about his pigeons. She complains that large numbers of them gather on her roof and that she cannot get her washing hung out for fear that it will be fouled by pigeon droppings. Eventually Hilda threatens to raise an action in nuisance seeking interdict to prevent Stan from keeping pigeons.*
    You are Stan's only friend and he seeks your advice.

Notes for answer
Clearly the facts resemble *Allison v. Stevenson*. However in this case a court might well reach a different conclusion and refuse interdict. There are significant distinguishing factors. While the court has to balance the conflicting interests of neighbours, in *Allison* there was material harm caused to roans and drainpipes. Inconvenience has to be substantial before it becomes actionable and Hilda's complaints appear lacking in substance. This may be a case for applying the maxim, *lex non favet votis delicatorum*, the law does not favour the wishes of the fastidious. If it is the case that Hilda's washing gets covered in guano whenever she hangs it out to dry then her case may be strengthened. Even so it is not obvious that an interdict will be granted. Everyone knows that the odd bird dropping is a natural hazard of drying washing outdoors. The text is deliberately vague on whether Hilda's washing has actually suffered to any extent. Although Stan may feel that his behaviour in keeping pigeons is reasonable this is not really the point. The critical issue is whether the harm or inconvenience suffered by Hilda is more than reasonably tolerable (*Watt v. Jamieson*). On the basis of the facts as set out in the text it must be highly doubtful whether the *plus quam tolerabile* test will be satisfied.
    In the unlikely event that the court holds that the inconvenience suffered by Hilda amounts to nuisance Stan cannot defend the action by arguing that he and his pigeons were there first. It is no defence to state that the petitioner came to the nuisance (*Webster v. Lord Advocate*). Furthermore Stan is not protected by prescription since he kept pigeons for only 10 years and the prescriptive period is 20 (Prescription and Limitation (Scotland) Act 1973, s.7(1)).
    You should advise Stan that it is most unlikely that he will have to give up his pigeons. Advise him to defend any action brought by Hilda on the basis that any inconvenience suffered by Hilda is insufficiently grave to amount to nuisance.

INDEX